WITH THIS RING

*Based On A True Story Of
Deception And Courage*

WITH THIS RING

Based On A True Story Of Deception And Courage

Sofia Rinehold

New Horizon Press   Far Hills, New Jersey

Requests for permission should be addressed to:
New Horizon Press
P.O. Box 669
Far Hills, NJ 07931

Rinehold, Sofia.
    With This Ring : Based on a true story of deception and courage

Library of Congress Catalog Card Number: 93-61693

ISBN: 0-88282-089-3
New Horizon Press

Manufactured in the U.S.A.

1998 1997 1996 1995 1994 / 5 4 3 2 1

I never appreciated the Stellar Star until I understood its place in bird society, that noisy, raucous, seemingly domineering bird feathered in brilliant blue and shiny black. His vigilance saves the life of thousands. His noisy cries warn of danger as well as the location of food. God bless its strident call. When I am gone I'd count my life well spent if someone said the same for me.

— Sofia Rinehold

Author's Note

This book is based on the experiences of Sofia Rinehold, and reflects her perceptions of the past, present, and future. The personalities, events, actions, and conversations portrayed within the story have been taken from her memory, extensive interviews, research, court documents, letters, personal papers, press accounts, and the memories of participants.

All names and some events have been altered to protect the privacy of individuals.

Contents

	Acknowledgments	xi
	Prologue	xiii
One	Past Impressions	1
Two	First Glances	5
Three	With This Ring	17
Four	Another Victim	25
Five	More Evidence	31
Six	The Feds	37
Seven	Michael's Daughter	43
Eight	Prison	49
Nine	Alicia's Story	55
Ten	A Change of Custody	59
Eleven	Disillusioned	67
Twelve	Second Bigamy Exposed	75
Thirteen	Poems of Darkness	87
Fourteen	Visitation Falters	95
Fifteen	Further Leads	103
Sixteen	Will the Real Michael DeLorenzo Please Stand Up	111
Seventeen	Mt. St. Helens	115
Eighteen	Gayle's Story	119
Nineteen	Moral Support	127
Twenty	The Witnesses Speak	141
Twenty–One	A New Victim	153
Twenty–Two	In Court	157
Twenty–Three	Something of a Victory, Something of a Defeat	181
Twenty–Four	Sounding the Call	197
Twenty–Five	Trial Postscript	205
Twenty–Six	The Club Members	207
	Afterword	215
	Bibliography	223

Acknowledgments

For their contributions to this book, I'd like to thank:

The fine staff at New Horizon Press and especially Joan Dunphy, Publisher, for her sensitivity and understanding of the issues in this story.

Natasha Kern; an agent who really knows the market.

Norma, Mike, Charles, Gordon, Robert, Pierre, The Wild Ones, Inc.; for being there.

My writer's group, family, and the steadfast friends who encouraged me along the way, including my "errant neighbors" and Marsha. This book belongs to all of you.

Prologue

The telephone's insistent noise startled me, breaking into my romantic daydreams about the trip to China my new husband Michael DeLorenzo and I were planning. Earlier that day Michael had told me to expect his call. We were finally about to leave after months of delay. It had to be him. I rushed to the phone and grabbed it up.

"Hello. Is this Sofia DeLorenzo?" a male voice asked.

"Yes," I answered hesitantly, not recognizing the voice on the line.

"This is Detective Perkins of the Berk County Sheriff's Office. Do you drive a blue BMW?"

I began to tremble. The question frightened me. Since Mike wrecked his Audi, he had been driving my car. I feared what the next words might be.

"Yes," I again replied anxiously.

There was a slight pause. "We have arrested Michael DeLorenzo." He cleared his throat. During the pause my heart skipped several beats. "For forgery and grand theft."

I gasped.

The trooper went on. "When we opened the trunk of your car we found a box containing your mail. None of it has been opened. The post dates go back as far as four months."

"How could that be?" I murmured incredulously. Why would Mike have my mail?

"You'd better come pick up your car before it gets towed."
He added softly, "Let me give you the address."

My mind raced for a logical explanation for what I'd just
heard. My hand shook as I took down the address he gave me. I
recognized it as the location of a low income housing development
in the neighboring town of Madison. "There were a lot of papers in
the apartment we found him in," the detective continued. "Various
documents and a typewriter. We think DeLorenzo was using the
apartment for some type of con operation. He has a criminal
background and served time at the state penitentiary." He paused
for a moment. "We also think he's married to more than one
person. I'm sorry."

I don't recall whether I said goodbye or not. I don't
remember much of that afternoon, except that I did go to reclaim
my car. I began looking through stacks of mail in disbelief. There
were bank statements showing my accounts overdrawn, months of
unpaid bills, and even letters to my family that I remembered
placing in the mailbox—one included a five hundred dollar check
to help my niece with her college tuition. I was numb. "The whole
thing doesn't make sense," I murmured. In fact it made no sense at
all. I considered myself a good judge of character. How could I
have totally misread Michael. Had I measured him against the
values and ethics I learned as a child? Did they make me
vulnerable? With a deep love of family and a trusting nature, I
could not conceive a person without conscience.

There are singular events that occur in a person's life that alter the direction permanently. Events that are fortunate or unfortunate. Some effect one physically, some emotionally, some spiritually. They set character and beliefs that mold us both internally and externally into the people we become as well as the one others see.

One of my earliest memories is running along the train tracks to find the pathway up to the trestle. I was nearly four years old. I was following the older children to a brick yard to get some clay to mold. Suddenly a train whistle sounded. I ran faster. The train whistle shrieked again. The silver monster bored down upon me. I ran as fast as I could. In front of me I saw the trestle. Up I went—out of harm's way. To this day I start at loud noises; never have I run that fast again—but I still take chances.

I learned fear.

At five, I sat in the comforting shelter of my father's lap not ten feet from the man who had raped me. A short while before, I had told my father the truth and he believed me. The man was my father's friend. He didn't know it as we made small talk, but my father had called the police. We were waiting for them to arrive. Glancing out the window, I silently watched the sheriff's car pull into our driveway.

I learned to believe in justice.

At ten, my family and I lived in the lush green Yakima Valley farming region and I spent much of my free time riding a horse. At school I befriended a girl named Dulcie. She was Mexican and had come to the valley with her family whom she said were farmers. Dulcie was staying at another classmate's ranch and begged me to come visit. When I did I was appalled. She and her family lived in a chicken coop. They were migrant farm workers. A single mattress lay on the dirty floor where the parents and their four small children slept. Finding out that human beings lived like that made me sick to my stomach. I resolved to do something about it.

I learned outrage.

My dear father died when I was twelve and my mother had to find a way to earn a living. We moved from the quiet serene country setting of my childhood to the city. While working to support us, my mother put herself through college. I was shy. Making friends at a new school was difficult, but I persevered. I attended eight schools between grades seven and twelve. One of the schools I attended, when I was fifteen, was St. Joseph's Academy for Girls in Yakima, Washington. It had a quiet academic atmosphere. Classes were taught by nuns in full habit. Debbie, one of the girls I met there, told me she had become involved with an unsavory man in her neighborhood. Debbie seemed a sweet girl, but I didn't know her well and was shocked that she confided in me. Later Debbie told me she'd been sent to recruit me. It was then I learned how easily people can be corrupted.

One Saturday she asked me to meet her downtown to go shopping. We hadn't been on the street five minutes when the man showed up. He took us to the country and made a lewd show of himself as well as brandishing a pistol he kept in his glove box. Disgusting and frightening, he offered to set me up with a local druggist. Determined to ensnare them, I agreed.

The moment I reached safety, I contacted my priest and a police detective. I helped them gather evidence and a successful prosecution followed. It was not until later, however, when a letter of commendation from the police detective arrived in the mail did my mother learn what happened.

I learned to keep my own counsel.

At eighteen, I fell in love with a boy who had joined the navy. We married despite my mother's and his family's concerns that we were too young. At first I followed him from port to port, but soon I became pregnant. Our baby girl was born healthy and happy, but when she was one year old she contacted meningitis. She was left profoundly deaf. My husband couldn't adjust to her handicap and, although by now we had another child, we drifted apart. Before my twentieth birthday we parted permanently. I was left alone to raise a deaf child.

I learned independence.

Raising a child alone is difficult. Raising a handicapped child alone is formidable. However, I resolved that my children, especially my eldest daughter, would have every opportunity to develop to their fullest potentials. I focused only on them and the job I needed to support them. I worked at night; so I could attend day classes at the Seattle Hearing and Speech Center for the PreSchool Deaf. There I learned to teach my deaf child so we could begin her education together. There was no one upon whom to lean or depend. My mother had remarried—her new husband was a college professor and they moved far away.

I learned fortitude.

Unexpectedly, I met a man who seemed happily secure—financially and emotionally. We married and had a child together. Although he loved the children, his and mine, he had poor parenting skills and took little interest in their activities. Still our marriage endured. He was a good provider, generous and kind. In this atmosphere I too became secure until the day, over fifteen years later, when he came to me to ask for a divorce. He wanted to marry someone else. I was crushed.

He made the arrangements and I cooperated. There was nothing else to do. During the divorce hearing, I barely paid attention until my lawyer, her voice rising suddenly, began a new vein of questioning parrying and pushing my husband. She handed him a slip of paper. It was a credit application to open a charge account. My lawyer began to ask him a series of questions about it. I couldn't understand why she was spending so much time on this subject which seemed so trivial. Then I noticed my husband becoming red faced and stammering his replies. I leaned closer to see and hear better. She was asking him about a person he had listed on the paper as his fiancee. I gasped at the name. It was his own sister.

The judge, who had been rocking back and forth on his chair, banged it down. He called my husband, my husband's lawyer, and mine to the bench; then he granted the divorce.

I learned disillusionment.

Gathering up the pieces of yourself after an unexpected divorce isn't easy. Gathering up those same pieces when your ego and self-worth have been so badly shattered is even harder. Slowly I tried to build a new life. I became involved in more activities to help the deaf. It was rewarding. My career blossomed. But I was lonely. Several years passed, and feeling very tired physically and mentally from a life which revolved solely around work and, of course, my children who were quickly growing up, I decided to take a trip to Europe.

During the trip I visited social centers for the deaf. I traveled alone. In Breindisi, a small port city in Southern Italy, a leather-clad man, who wanted to rob me, threatened me with a pistol. In just moments, the thin protective layer that I had woven around myself and my feelings since the divorce unraveled. Suddenly, I realized how isolated and solitary I had become—how frightening life could be without someone to love and protect you.

I learned vulnerability.

I also had become the perfect candidate to be a victim.

Attractive, refined, intelligent brunette 38. Single mom, financially secure, seeks kind, strong, successful gentleman, 40-50 for whom commitment, family values, the arts, music, outdoors sports and children are important, as is the ability to care deeply for someone. Letter/Photo 4282.

◆

If anyone had predicted five years before that sometime in the near future I would be placing an advertisement in the personal column of a newspaper, I would have smiled and thought them more than slightly deranged. However, the twists of fate are many and often they upset both our self-image and our certainty. So it was with that feeling, rather chagrined and not a little humbled by this realization, I phoned the Portland Journal, our local newspaper, to place this ad which my children had helped me write.

I told them and myself not to expect miracles; after all I was not a young, romantic, adventurous girl anymore, but a mature sophisticated woman who had seen and learned more than her share of life's bittersweet lessons. Still, I must admit I found myself slightly giddy and expectant waiting for replies.

To my surprise there were quite a few. As I looked through them, one particularly seemed to embody most of the qualities I had been hoping against hope to find in a man.

Harricort, The Small Development Company
With The Big Company Savvy
Padget, Bermuda

At 6'4", 212 lbs, I'm neither petite nor a giant. Handsome? We all define that on a personal basis. Let's say, probably safely, good looking, not fat. Big frame, reasonably muscular. Not a health nut and don't jog. Expert skiing, locally at Mount Hood, swimming, other sports like riding horses, good diet, health habits, keep me fit.

I have a well-defined value system, so none of the fears that weave throughout the weekly ads really apply; i.e. drugs, alcohol, disease—all that—it's not my style. My needs are simple: honesty, values, caring, trust, sharing, cherishing, all so easy to specify—and so difficult to find.

I've long lost my intensity for material things; drive a classic Eldorado and a nearly new Audi. Last year I sold the 52' Chris Craft (memories took the joy away). Sequentially, I owned five single engine aircraft and one twin-engine plane, but have left that too, at least for a while. And my then twin-engine pilot went to work flying for Nordstrom Toys, but they had their time and place. It may be important to you that I have all my hair.

Family: I've fathered four, three out on their own. My daughter, still with me, will be 12 in June, is borderline gifted, lovely, sweet, and is lucky enough to have a nice lady live-in tutor, credentialed, so we can travel.

I run a low-profile real estate development firm and co-own another. We do luxury ($2 mil & up) residential developments, small shopping centers, office buildings, mostly in Bermuda, so we ricochet to the Islands often. My firms are small, uncluttered, successful.

Education/other: Standard (BS); U of Texas (MBA); Wharton (26 weeks for intermediate and advanced management courses); US Navy (52 months; emerged as Lt. (jg), submarine service).

I'm older than you are, but not significantly so. My conclusion is that the single life is not for me and would like to cut short, sensibly, the process of correcting that situation. I've read the Portland Journal for years, noticed the ads with amusement, but yours caught my eye and I'm taking a flyer. I've had one relationship since dissolution: a 40-year-old MD/psychiatrist/attorney/heiress/jet setter. She fell in love; I didn't; the jet set thing isn't my style either. I've been there and back. I love music—from classics to jazz to country to soft rock; am a voracious reader/book collector; enjoy work, travel, family, companionship—an uncomplicated life without pretense, theater.

"The ball's in your court." Give me a call at home (unlisted) or a note to the office (attached letterheads). Home: 458-0332; daughter may answer (no matter). Mark note to office personal.

Michael DeLorenzo
DIV
-of-
Harricort Investment Inc.
Investment Developments
813 Plaza 80, Portland 98102

On a Tuesday evening in early April, after a particularly wearying day at my work as a Purchasing Agent for an import/manufacturing firm, where everyone else was either married or twentyish and single, I gathered up my courage. I picked up the telephone and dialed Michael DeLorenzo's home number. Perhaps it was fate or just whimsical luck, but a deep male voice answered. It radiated masculinity, attractiveness, and most of all security.

"Hello, this is Michael DeLorenzo. May I be of some help?"

"Perhaps," I said softly, "This is Sofia Rinehold. You answered my advertisement in the Portland Journal."

"Sofia, what a lovely name. It suits the person I felt you'd be. I'm so glad you called. Would you like to get together?"

I took a deep breath. He seemed so outgoing, so easy to talk to.

"Yes," I managed.

"Well," he said, "I'm not busy, just sorting through some papers for a meeting tomorrow. Unimportant busy work really," he laughed a warm guileless sound. "If you're free why don't I come over and pick you up? I could take you out for a cup of coffee, so next time we meet it won't be one of those awful stomach-knotting first dates when neither person knows what to say."

Somehow I uttered a second, "Yes. That would be lovely." I gave him my address.

"I'll be over in less than thirty minutes," he said.

Within twenty minutes there was a knock on my front door. My face flushed, my hands trembling, I quickly walked over, opened it, and looked into the most charismatic blue eyes I'd ever seen. My eyes swept over the rest of him: a tall, well-built man with dark wavy hair just touched by gray. As I looked back in his eyes, his gaze locked with mine. "Are you ready?" he asked in that magnetic voice.

I nodded, not trusting myself to speak.

He took me to a little Italian cafe I'd never known existed, although it wasn't far from my house. Then he ordered us both orange cappuccino which burnt my mouth with bitter sweetness. Then we began to talk. My shyness evaporated as Michael drew me out. Gentle yet probing, he seemed to want to know everything about me; my past, my dreams, my thoughts and aspirations, what I want in life. Surprising myself, I even told him about the poetry I wrote in private and the books I hoped to write someday. "I really would like to do a book about Jeanette, my oldest daughter, and the challenges for a hearing person in raising a deaf child. I want to share what I learned with others facing the same task so they won't feel overwhelmed."

His eyes glistened as he said, "What a wonderful thing to want to do. You seem to love all your children so much, but I can see Jeanette is very special to you."

I smiled, "You're right, she is."

"Sofia, you're such a talented beautiful person, I'm so glad I answered that advertisement. I've never done anything like that before, but then, I'm sure you never placed one before."

I nodded my head and felt my face flushing.

He leaned closer to me and patted my hand, not in a flirtatious way, but as if to encourage me to tell him more. I did. I found myself totally confiding in him the feelings I had kept within me for so long, all the time locked in the magic of his penetrating blue eyes. Listening intently, he seemed to shut out the rest of the world and concentrate only on me.

Finally, when he was sure I had told him everything I wanted to say, he began to talk about himself.

"I wish I could tell you I've lived my life with the wisdom and compassion you've shown in the face of so much adversity. I wish I could, but I can't."

I started to object. "I can already see you're one of the most sensitive people I've ever met."

He smiled wistfully but shook his head, "I wish that were so, but let me tell you about it. I'll try to be as forthcoming as you have been."

I could see there were things he needed to say and kept silent.

"You know from my letter that I've been married before. My first wife's name is Anna. We were together a long time, have four wonderful children who I am still very close to, but then I had one of those short mid-life flings everyone is always talking about." He paused, grimacing. "I was stupid, very stupid and then." For the first time he looked away from me at some invisible spot on the ceiling. A few moments later he went on. "The woman became pregnant. My wife divorced me and I felt such guilt and responsibility, I married the other woman. It only lasted a short time. She was unfit to be a mother," he said bitterly. "I'll tell you about her sometime. The only thing good to come out of it is my beautiful daughter Maria who is now twelve and lives with me."

Not giving me any time to reply, he rushed on. "After the second divorce, when I was left alone to raise my daughter, I felt desperate and lonely and I keenly missed family life which has always been so important to me. I rushed into another relationship to give my daughter a mother. That too was a mistake and didn't last."

"Meanwhile my career has prospered. I'm in land development as I wrote you and have a wonderful business partner. We've done very well together." He blushed, "I'm a millionaire many times over. I have a palatial home in Bermuda where I travel for business often in my private plane. I boat around the islands or race our sports cars with some..." he smiled sheepishly, "movie star friends. Because I must for business reasons, I travel constantly to exotic places. I ski, swim, and revel in the outdoors, but when I get home I am more lonely than ever. Because of my traveling and long hours, Maria is staying with my partner's girlfriend, a multi-millionaire named Catherine. At least I know she's living in a luxurious mansion and is well cared for," he said, biting his lip pensively. "Since she has a live-in tutor, she doesn't go to public school. I can take them with me to Bermuda, where I have business, and other places. We are together often, but it isn't like living in a family. I miss so many little things; rites of passage as she's growing up, and events you can never see again once they have passed." He appeared to have finished his words about the past.

Once again he leaned toward me, "I hope I haven't disappointed you," he said sadly, "but I wanted to tell you everything. I want us to begin without illusions, in an atmosphere of truth. Otherwise, it will all mean nothing."

"Agreed," I said gently. "And I'm not disappointed or disillusioned. We both bring our pasts—whatever they have been—to this moment. They've made us what we are today. If you can accept mine, I can accept yours."

"Freely and thankfully," he said.

◆

As our relationship deepened and I got to know him in the two months that followed, Michael seemed to be more and more the person of whom I had always dreamed. As we dined, danced, picnicked, and just spent time alone, or with our families, or friends, my wonderment at finding this strong but gentle man grew. Perhaps all the heartaches and disappointments in my earlier life had a purpose—so that I would be ready to relish and appreciate the love developing between us.

I met Michael's daughter, Maria, for the first time during this period. A beauty with deep brown eyes and blond hair, she seemed as sweet and giving as Michael had told me. She confirmed the stories about her living in a mansion, having a tutor, the home in Bermuda, movie star connections, and other such things.

It was very soon afterward, on a cool morning as we hiked in an alpine meadow that Michael asked me to marry him. "Of course," I immediately replied and added, "Yes, yes."

As mist rose in the early sunlight, he clasped me in his arms and said, "To our new beginning." Never had I felt so safe as in his arms. Tears welled in my eyes as I repeated his words to myself.

◆

The plans Michael made for our marriage seemed too wonderful to be real and we shared them first with my children. After telling Maria together, Michael wrote to the rest of his family.

~ Michael DeLorenzo ~

Dear children, friends, relatives, and other loved ones:

Some of you are already aware of my personal good news, and Maria's, but I can't resist sharing it with all of you.

Not long ago, as time passes on it's fleeting wings, it was my good fortune to meet a lady whose beauty, grace, loveliness, and delicate nature captured my heart—and Maria's as well.

I've fallen under her spell. She reciprocates my feelings. We are going to be married shortly at Somerset, Bermuda. Then, at the Princess Hotel's beach, in Bermuda, the vows will be repeated in a traditional native ceremony.

In addition to being a woman of exceptional exquisiteness and picturesqueness, externally, she is delicate, lovely, and soft-spoken.

She has many talents. Far more than I. She is more than I deserve but perhaps I can live up to her expectations. If so, then it will all even out.

She does have a name, but we'll get to that later. . .

Among her many qualities and talents are:

A genuine love of all people, poor or affluent, handsome or misshapen, kind or selfish, generous or greedy.

She appreciates beauty in all its forms. She is cultured in the finest sense of the definition.

She is an accomplished writer/author of poetry, short stories for children of all ages, and is in the last stages of completing the definitive text for parents of deaf or otherwise handicapped children—a biography written in novel form, so the reader can experience the life of the subject as she, in fact, lived it.

She listens, plays, understands, feels, music with the same enthusiasm and inspiration with which she writes. First love, opera, followed by the music of French composers, folk, jazz, blue grass and contemporary.

Loving nature as she does, it is not surprising that she can reproduce it on canvas in all forms, with sensitivity, understanding, and expression, the nuances and shadings of nature, man and beast, in the natural or raw, crisp beauty of the subject, whatever it may be. She is with brush as she is with the ivory keys or song.

The complete woman, mother, she is Sofia (Sof-i-ya) Rinehold, soon to be Mrs. Michael DeLorenzo. I'm luckier than I deserve, some of you will agree all too heartily. In summary, she is a woman to cherish. . .

                         Dad/Michael

I too wrote or introduced Michael to family and friends. One of them, Billy Amer, a gentle deaf young man was very close to us and quickly became friends with Maria and Michael.

Two weeks before the wedding date I was searching for the perfect dress. The Linen Source didn't have the reception invitations I really wanted; so I had to take my second choice, but as I walked out of the shop the sky was a heavenly blue, birds were singing, flowers in bloom and my spirits had never been higher. Michael had gone out to price a new car that day. He had crashed his the week before—I attributed it to the excitement which made it so difficult to concentrate on mundane matters like working, driving, eating, breathing, etc. . .

I felt dizzily happy, but as the wedding date drew closer my nervousness grew. When I called my mother with the news of the date of the big day she was strangely anxious. "I hope you won't fall on your face with this marriage," she said softly.

"What do you mean?" I asked warily. She refused to go on and I hung up feeling disturbed, but I chalked it up to old age pessimism. At least my sisters and daughters felt as jubilantly as I did. They were constantly wishing me joy—the joy and happiness they said I deserved.

A week before the ceremony, awful pre-wedding jitters set in. Michael told me that transportation costs to fly the family to Bermuda first class, the only way he wanted them to go, were a lot more than he anticipated—$17,000. Just thinking of that kind of expenditure made me even more nervous—as if a sudden storm dissipated the balmy weather.

Two days before we were to leave for Bermuda, disaster occurred. That morning, papers arrived by courier. Michael said he was being sued for something his ex-wife had cosigned and she wouldn't relinquish Maria's passport until Michael paid. We stared at each other in disbelief. "That awful woman has ruined my life again," Michael scowled angrily. "It isn't enough that she almost injured our daughter."

Forgetting our own problem I said, "What happened, Michael?"

He shook his head, "When Maria was about four years old I had to break down her mother's apartment door just as her mother was about to harm Maria."

"What a terrible memory for you both to have," I said sympathetically and hugged him to me. I went on, "Darling I don't care about the trip. We'll go to Bermuda later. The only thing that really matters is what we have now." His face brightened.

"You're right, of course. Our marriage is the important thing. I'll take you on an even more wonderful trip afterward."

We changed all our plans and went to Portland to obtain our marriage license. I had a knot in my stomach but felt much better once the license was in our hands.

We celebrated at Oscar's, a romantic seafood restaurant in the marina. We held hands, looked out on the serene sea and just enjoyed being with each other. With tears in his eyes, Michael said, "Sofia, you'll never know how much I love you."

"And I you," I replied. It was so wonderful to have someone care for me after all this time alone.

A few days later, on June 15, we made arrangements for our wedding in front of Joshua Henley, a judge in Portland. The wedding would take place the next day at 4:00 P.M.

On June 16, we were finally married. When Michael kissed me after the ceremony, I realized once again that the place and time didn't matter, only the happiness we both felt at finally being husband and wife.

◆

Since our wedding trip was postponed, we went to pick up Maria who had asked to live with us. To my amazement, instead of going to a mansion, we went to an apartment at 140th and 8th streets in downtown Portland. It was a low income housing complex.

Maria's possessions consisted of a very cheap, worn, bedroom set, an old broken desk, a television set with video games, and a few boxes of clothes. When I turned to Michael for an explanation he put his fingers to his lips. "Shush," he said secretively. "I'll tell you later about what happened."

I did not want to embarrass Maria. I really did not want to know. I never mentioned it again and neither did he.

Maria and I became fast friends. She was a loving child. She made me presents and began to confide in me her thoughts about her birthmother, the trust fund she was to receive at age twenty-one, and the mansion where she lived but had to leave overnight when her father's partner and his mistress broke up. "Thank goodness you told me that," I murmured. Maria looked at me strangely.

Meanwhile, the trip Michael and I were supposed to take to Bermuda kept on being put off. Finally, Mike came home one night and asked me, "How would you like to go to the Orient instead? Partially on business."

Delighted to travel, I agreed.

"My partners and I will set the date," Michael said. I waited anxiously, but that trip too kept getting postponed.

One day Michael took me to visit the beautiful site of a building he was erecting. "This is for us my darling," he said as he gestured toward the hills and explained his plans. I was overcome by the beauty and grandeur of the exclusive setting.

"Michael, I don't know what to say, it's so incredible."

"You don't have to say anything, Sofia," he said looking at me lovingly. "Just being my wife says it all."

Later, when we got home and he gave me the blueprints, I looked at them and was somewhat surprised. I knew something about architecture and the foundation at the building site looked different from the way Michael had described it. But knowing builders often change their original plans due to conditions they find, I didn't mention it. I didn't want to seem like I was nagging and questioning the wonderful surprise he had given me.

That night Michael had me sign an application card for a joint bank account. He preferred to have me put him on mine, but for some reason I refused. The next day, he brought bank cards home for a joint account and I signed them.

While we waited for our trip to the Orient, we went to Montana to ski Flathead Peaks. I was looking forward to skiing with Michael because he had told me he always skied expert runs. I too was an advanced skier. When I watched him for the first time, however, his skills seemed poor at best and he limped back to me saying he'd turned his ankle. Knowing that most men didn't like women beating them at sports, I said nothing. Later, I went out to get some equipment from the trunk of his car and saw some checks stuffed into a glove there. Plucking them out I was surprised to see they were imprinted with his and his ex-wife's name and were current. When I asked him about them that night, Michael made light of it. I quickly forgot the incident when I discovered my camera was gone and almost all the photographs of our first trip together disappeared with it. I was crestfallen.

"The pictures are in here Sofia," Michael said, tapping his heart. "They'll never fade or tear or get stolen there. They'll always be ours to keep." Looking at him, I sighed. Once again the true sensitivity of this man I had married struck me.

◆

And then the phone call came from the police about Michael's criminal past. Now I was astounded and despondent. How could those awful allegations be true: Michael a thief, a forger, and even more shocking—a bigamist?

The moment the detective called, all of my dreams and plans for the future fell apart.

As I lay in bed that night, my mind raced from one enigma to another. Thinking of the present was horrendous and the past plagued me. Mike had been arrested for forgery and grand theft. He had presented himself to me as a successful businessman, well educated, a devoted family man who wanted a loving wife and a mother for his twelve-year-old daughter, Maria.

Sleepless, I reviewed our time together. Whenever Michael discussed his life, whether he was talking about his business travels, lifestyle, living accommodations, or people he ostensibly knew, Maria gave no indication that the stories were untrue. My thoughts turned to his daughter. Letters she wrote to her friends were full of the same stories of living in Bermuda, traveling with a private tutor, and living a life of privilege. She was charming. I might have suspected an adult of lying but never a child—certainly not a young girl who made me tiny origami baskets and confided in me.

I began to go back over the last three months, carefully searching for clues. I thought of the stories Mike had told me of skiing the more challenging runs on Mount Hood. But when we took that trip to Montana, I had been keenly disappointed after the first run. He was a mediocre skier and could not ski advanced runs. Then there were the checks I found in the trunk of his car. Although I was distressed, he had made light of still having checks on a joint account with his "former" wife. By the time we left the resort I had forgotten all about it. I was more occupied with the distress of having had my camera stolen.

When we got back, Michael continued to come home with one excuse after another why our new trip was postponed. As time went on my anger increased at the business and personal problems standing in our way. Several times I had started to wonder if Mike was lying as to the reasons but always I repressed the thought.

Suddenly, a strange incident came to mind. I remembered waking in the middle of the night the week before this. Michael was standing by our bedroom window leaning on the sill, tears in his eyes and on his cheeks. When I asked him what was the matter he said, "The only mistake I made was falling in love with you. Now, I wonder how long it will be before you throw me out of the house." It's true I had become frustrated with him, but why this? I could not understand why the man I had come to think of as so mature, so reliable, would become so strangely overly emotional.

Looking back now I feel Michael must have known his arrest was imminent. As I went over the past few days in my memory, his attitude the night he wept began to make more sense to me. Mike had really been spending time preparing me, softening me with stories of his fear of abandonment and dependency on his mother during the Depression. With the shock of sudden understanding, I saw the connection between what he had told me and the hold he had over his daughter, Maria. She lived in fear that he might commit suicide. Maria had confided in my daughter, Irene. "He told me if we were ever separated he would kill himself. I have to take care of him."

Mike had intended his expressions of fears as a hook to make me sympathize with any trouble he might get into, but years of struggling and raising a disabled child had made me understand real adversity and struggling. I had learned that it was possible to surmount hardship without abandoning ones principles, hopes and dreams. But after the police called, my dreams of marital happiness vanished. I was disgusted with him, not sympathetic.

He had, without even giving me a second thought, taken away any security I had. Bills were unpaid, and I was in danger of losing my home. Now I had to fight to get my life together if I was to survive. I had to telephone a dozen creditors. The hardest call would be the one to the mortgage company. They were threatening foreclosure on my house for nonpayment. As I went through every conceivable option, I determined that the only way to avoid bankruptcy was to experience a miracle. I sighed heavily. There was no one to make it happen. I'd have to create it myself.

As I lay tossing in bed, I could think only of my predicament. I waited hours for sleep to come. It was nearly 3:00 A.M. when the telephone rang again. I still hadn't slept. "Hello," I answered in a tired voice.

"This is Michael." He paused for a moment as if waiting for me to say something. I was silent.

Finally, I spoke. "I had a call from the police. They said you're in jail. They told me a lot of other things too," I replied darkly.

"You sound upset. I don't blame you for being upset but I can explain. . ."

My anger exploded. I didn't wait for him to finish. "No, Michael, I don't think you can. You see, you can't explain away being a criminal or a bigamist. It's just not explainable."

"Can I come home? Would you bail me out?" he begged. "Please, please."

Listening to his whining pleas, hours of repressed feelings sprang to the surface. I knew there was no way I could be sympathetic, not after what he'd done. My anger burst into white heat. "You got yourself in jail," I snapped. "You can damn well get yourself out."

I hung up the telephone without waiting for a reply and lay there feeling my anger translate itself into rope-tight muscles. I knew tomorrow was going to be a tough day, perhaps the toughest I had ever faced. Tired or not, I was going to have to make a lot of decisions. I tried to calm myself but still couldn't sleep. As I lay there, my head aching, I kept asking myself what possessed Mike to do this to me. I had been hurt before but couldn't remember ever having had an enemy; it seemed impossible that I could have married one.

An hour or two before dawn, I finally fell asleep. When I awoke, light was creeping across the sky. I placed a call to a long time friend, Seth Baker, and explained what had happened. He hurried over and helped me prepare an updated resume. We made a number of copies at the library and mailed them. Seth reminded me that I had a good many friends and gave me some badly needed encouragement.

After he left I felt better. I gathered my courage and telephoned the Personnel Director at Ryan Electronics, Incorporated. Rachel Ward had offered me a job there several years ago and though I declined it, we periodically touched base. I told her that I was having marital problems and I had mailed her a resume. She said, "Could you bring me one today? I have a job I'd like you to interview for tomorrow." I couldn't believe my luck and rushed over. I was hired as a customer service representative the following day.

Later I received another surprising phone call. This one was from Alicia, Michael's third wife. She only asked one question, "Are Michael and you married?"

I answered, "Yes."

She replied, "Oh my God," and hung up.

◆

The more difficult problems I faced one at a time. I dealt with bill collectors and my mortgage company. I opened a credit line to pay at least some of my bills. I moved quickly because I knew soon no one would extend me credit. Strangers would be less understanding of my plight than members of my family and close friends. Perhaps the most difficult task was telling Michael's daughter, Maria, that her father was in jail.

We went for a long walk together, as much for my comfort level as for hers. It's difficult to discuss wrenching topics facing one another seated on rigid chairs. Walking side by side gives a measure of naturalness. Quietly, I told her about her father. Maria was plainly scared. She admitted that most, if not all, of the things I'd been told by Michael before his arrest had no element of truth. As I listened I became more appalled. Virtually every fragment of the life he'd presented was a fabrication. I could not help asking her, "Why did you lie for him?"

"Dad told me I would be disloyal if I didn't agree with what he said, that I was too young to understand it now, but that some day I would. I knew it was wrong but I didn't know what else to do." Maria's eyes filled with tears. I knew she was afraid of what might happen to her father if they were separated. Knowing this, I tried to be as gentle as possible with her.

When Michael got out of jail he came to my house. "Just collect your personal effects and leave," I said dejectedly. "Maria is welcome to stay here until you can find a place for her," I went on. I didn't tell him that I had already telephoned his son, Michael Jr., who had refused to give Maria sanctuary, as had Maria's two half-sisters. The grown children Michael had always claimed were so close and dear to him had, in reality, never met Maria and refused to have anything to do with their father. Their rejection of Maria seemed to me especially sad since no one seemed to know, or care, where her real mother could be reached.

A week later I came home from work to find Maria gone. When I went to sleep that night it was with a sense of relief, rather than loss. Though I was worried about what would happen to Maria, she had sulked continuously since her father's eviction. After talking with him she had turned sullen. Not knowing who to blame she ended up blaming her father's misfortune on me.

Yet even though I was relieved, I could not stop thinking of her. Who would take care of her? How would she grow up with a father who not only stole and forged but constantly fed her lies?

Several months passed before Michael was rudely pushed back into my life. My daughter Irene telephoned, and she was frantic. "Mom, you won't believe this. I just found out that Michael and Maria moved in with Billy Amer."

I couldn't believe it. Billy, who was deaf, was gentle and trusting. As close to us as family, he had also been kind to Michael and Maria. I felt sick. "We have to warn Billy. I don't know what else we can do." I replied. I felt ashamed and sickened that my husband, the pariah, had gained access to my friends and family through me. "How can I protect them?" I wondered.

I telephoned Michael. Maria answered the telephone. Her father must have instructed her that he didn't want to talk. I told her if she didn't get him on the phone right away I was going to get in my car and drive up there. He may even have been listening; he came right on the line. I warned Michael if he did anything, even the slightest little thing to Billy, he was going to pay for it. Furthermore, I told him I was going to tell Billy's landlord all about him. I would tell the man how crooked Michael is so he could watch Michael too. And I was going to call the Portland Police Department so they would know where Michael was living.

I went on, "You better not even breathe wrong because all of us are going to be watching you."

Michael DeLorenzo and Maria moved shortly after that while Billy Amer was at work. Michael left without paying Billy for his half of the rent. Michael returned a week or so later. He wanted Billy to ask me for the wedding rings Michael had given me. I wondered why he was so desperate to get them.

A few weeks later I found out the reason. I learned that Michael DeLorenzo appeared in Portland district court. The rings he'd been seeking had been purchased with a check he had written on a closed account. That, however, was a minor point. Michael had also forged a letter on the stationery of a Portland physician. His intent was to avoid incarceration. It described an advanced state of cancer (adenocarcinoma) from which Michael announced he suffered. Deputy Prosecutor Gordon, smelling a rat, called Dr.

Cooper. The doctor later viewed the letter and said the signature was his, but "the contents were totally fabricated," and the typing on the letter was not his. The doctor had treated the defendant for a minor problem. The defendant, after being advised by his attorney, Andrew Galveston, that he was "busted," wrote a letter admitting the forgery. Later, in open court, Michael apologized to the Court for his forgery and fraud. He was given nine months in jail.

Knowing Michael was in jail made me feel safer, more confident, and softened the effect of the depravation and pain his lies and thievery brought to my life. Time passed and I thought my awful experiences with Michael were over.

Months later I had a visit from a fellow writer, Bart Hager. Bart had met Michael at my home, shortly after we married. Bart told me, "I saw Michael with a woman a few weeks ago. They were standing outside a Catholic service on Easter Sunday. " Bart paused and then, staring at me, went on. "I think he was wearing a wedding band. He became nervous when he recognized me, made a quick excuse, and slipped back inside the church, though he had just emerged for a cigarette. Seeing me obviously spooked him. I guess he was worried I might tell someone the truth about him."

That unexpected meeting still bothered Bart. We spent a lot of time talking about what should be done. I encouraged him to go to the parish priest and tell him about Michael's criminal background and his bigamy. "Someone needs to sound the alarm and alert that woman," I said.

Bart nodded, "I've watched for her ever since that service but I haven't see her again."

After Bart left, thinking about the incident disturbed me. I tried but I couldn't seem to put it out of my mind.

I found out later that Michael had already picked out a new target. The woman's name was Gayle Higgins.

At this point, my own financial problems were overwhelming. To save anything, I had to work a demanding schedule. After a while though, I realized it was probably good for me. With the nonstop work, I thought less and less about Michael unless someone mentioned him. More than a year passed before Michael DeLorenzo and his daughter crossed my path again. But when the time came, it was with a vengeance.

The voice on the phone was soft and feminine. "Sofia?" the person said, "this is Jennifer. Jennifer Surel. Maria's mother." She paused and I heard a deep intake of breath. Then she rushed on, "I know you've heard awful things about me from Michael, but they are all untrue."

"Jennifer, there is no one more ready to believe that than I am."

"Thank you, Sofia. This is so difficult, but I desperately need your help."

Hearing the pain in her voice, I broke in as gently as I could, "Jennifer, I'm sure you can understand that I'm trying to forget I ever knew Michael and to get my own life back together. A life, I must add, he almost destroyed with his lies and thievery." I described some of my experiences with Michael for her.

"Of course, I understand how you feel," she said slowly when I finished. Then her voice strengthened, "but I know you cared so much about my daughter."

"Yes I did," I agreed.

"It's her life with Michael that I need to talk to you about. Please, could I see you?"

The thought of Michael with that poor child gave me shivers. Before I could ponder Jennifer's request, I heard myself saying, "All right Jennifer, come tomorrow night about eight."

I had mixed feelings as I opened my door the next evening. Jennifer and I stared at one another for several moments, assessing and comparing what we saw with what we had imagined, or been told by Michael.

She was a tall, almost waifish, tawny blond, with the ponytail and well scrubbed, pretty look of a college cheerleader—not at all what I had expected.

"Calling you was one of the hardest things I've ever done," Jennifer began. "Knowing the terrible lies Michael has told so many people about me, I was afraid you'd just say, 'You bitch,' and hang up. I didn't know what to expect. So few people have been willing to help me."

Once we sat down and Jennifer told me her own experiences, I could see why she grasped for any possible help. "I've been separated from my child since she was five," she said tearfully.

"Jennifer, how did you meet Michael?"

"I applied for a job at Greatfield, his company, and was hired immediately. It was a great relief as my responsibilities weighed heavily upon me. I enjoyed the job and most of the people I met there. Within a few weeks, I was treated as an old friend by the staff and was personally invited by Michael DeLorenzo, my new boss, to join a small group which met almost daily after work at the Thunderbird Hotel for drinks and hors d'oeuvres. They had their own table and the sky was the limit. The company paid the bill. During this time I became well acquainted with the company's Vice President, Ernie Pace and also Allan Pace."

"That must have made you feel good?" I murmured.

She nodded. "I enjoyed their company because the conversation was lively, and I was openly impressed by Michael DeLorenzo's intelligence. I had always loved listening to a brilliant man talk."

"I know how that one gets you," I smiled.

"Being around someone like that made me feel that I could be more than what I was. Somehow I felt I would grow just from the exposure. It was exciting. I was frankly delighted that they seemed to accept me into their group.

"I had worked for Greatfield for about a month when Michael asked me to join him and several of his regular companions, at a celebration at The Rustic restaurant. I really didn't want to go. I had things at home which needed my attention but he wouldn't take no for an answer. 'Please Jennifer,' Michael pressed, 'I really want you to come with me. This is a very big celebration and I also have something I want to show you.'"

Jennifer bowed her head. "He drove me to his house on the waterfront. It was quiet and lovely, set far off the street next to the lake. The home was silent. Our footsteps echoed on the marble entry way as we entered. The interior was quiet and beautiful. 'It's just been redecorated, Jennifer, how do you like it?' Michael asked. 'Very much,' I said. I had seen the decorator's bills at the office, they were enormous. The results were apparent.

"Just being in such a lovely home was an exciting experience. After Michael changed into a dress suit, he led me out to his dock. We cruised for an hour or so in his yacht and dined at a dockside restaurant. We talked for hours. He just sat there gazing at me, absorbing everything I said."

"How original," I interjected.

"I felt closer to him than I had to any man in my life, and I was extremely flattered by his attention to me. As we cruised back toward his home, he continued to press me for more details of my life. I told him things I had never confessed to anyone else."

I sighed.

"When the evening was nearly over and we were nearing my home, Michael suddenly asked me, 'Do you think you could love me?' It was so unexpected I didn't reply. He continued without my answer. 'I'm a very successful businessman and one of the attributes that contributes to my success is making quick decisions, and they are never wrong. I've made a decision,' he declared. 'You are going to marry me.'"

Jennifer shook her head again. "Once the shock wore off, I started laughing, thinking he couldn't possibly be serious. But he was. 'Well, you know I have a lot to offer you and your child,' he

said. "You can fall in love with a rich man as easily as a poor one. I
made this decision and I love you. I'll make all of your dreams
come true, I promise you. Will you just give me a chance? That's
all I ask, just give me a chance.'

"I thought, what do I have to lose? I felt like I was on a magic
carpet ride from that evening on. Michael falling in love with me so
quickly and completely swept me off my feet. His pursuit
intensified. He started taking me out almost every night. He sent
me flowers all the time. He called me several times daily. I don't
think I was alone more than four hours a day, seven days a week
from that time on. It was nice, but constant pressure. I became so
overwhelmed I wasn't thinking straight.

"Here was this wonderful, caring, solid person, who was
really concerned about my child. He worked long hours, a
reflection of the work ethic with which I was raised. He was a great
conversationalist. I thrived on the attention. Sometimes, when I
had a little time to myself, I'd get nervous. There was a large
difference in our ages, and he drank more than I would have liked.
If I would say that I didn't want to see him, he would become even
more attentive. He knew how to get to me," she said.

"We started traveling together. We would fly to Mexico for
the weekend in his private jet, or to Las Vegas for dinner. One time
Michael gave a party for me at the Oregon Athletic Club in
Hillsdale. He reserved a private room in the lavish setting. Waiters
hovered around us serving drinks called cannonballs; champagne
with a vodka chaser. For a young woman just turning thirty, it was
very seductive—irresistible."

The rest of their courtship was equally thrilling. Jennifer tried
to follow his every suggestion and order. Handling people was
something Michael prided himself on and he was good at it. Very
good. So when Jennifer told him she was pregnant, he decided she
would just have to get an abortion, that's all. Handling Jennifer,
Michael maintained, would be no problem at all.

However, Jennifer hadn't acted as she had been programmed. Instead she opted to have her baby and this caused the final breech in Michael's first marriage.

Anna, Michael's wife, insisted on a divorce. Michael had other serious problems with the law on his mind by this time. Because of them he needed to show he had a stable home.

Michael began to seriously consider marrying Jennifer Surel.

Two official looking gentlemen came to see Michael at his office one day. "Mr. Michael DeLorenzo?" the taller gray haired man asked.

"Yes," Michael replied, motioning them into his office.

Special agents George Harrington and Arthur Fielding introduced themselves and showed him their credentials. Special Agent Harrington spoke first.

"As a special agent, one of my functions is to investigate the possibility of criminal violations of the Internal Revenue laws and related offenses.

"In connection with my investigation of your tax liability [or other matter] I would like to ask you some questions. However, first I advise you that under the fifth amendment to the Constitution of the United States I cannot compel you to answer any questions or to submit any information if such answers or information might tend to incriminate you in any way. I also advise you that anything which you say and any documents you submit may be used against you in any criminal proceeding which may be undertaken. I advise you further that you may, if you wish, seek the assistance of an attorney before responding.

"Do you understand these rights?" Harrington asked.

Michael DeLorenzo displayed no outward sign of nervousness. He indicated that he understood the rights as they had been read and wished to continue the interview.

Agent Fielding consulted his notes and then looked Michael directly in the eye, "We have been unable to locate the filing of your returns for the last three years. Did you file for those years?"

"I believe I did. In fact I am sure that I prepared them myself."

"You are sure you filed for those years?" Fielding asked for reaffirmation.

"Yes," Michael replied. "My company accountants were Miles Henderson and later Pringley Bowles, but they did not prepare the returns."

Harrington showed DeLorenzo other previous forms. Michael identified signatures on those returns to be his.

"Could you please tell us your current address Mr. DeLorenzo?" Fielding asked politely.

"My current address is 39 East Water Street, Portland; I've lived there for two years. My house cost $90,000; I paid thirty-three percent down, borrowing the payment from Greatfield Corporation."

He went on to give a recounting of his recent business history with a lot of emphasis given to his success in building. It was one of Michael's favorite topics.

The agents asked DeLorenzo what his personal income source has been for the last four years. He stated his only income has been a salary from the corporation, but in order to determine how much, he'd have to go back to the applicable return to find out. He stated he had no nontaxable sources of revenues during this period from gifts and inheritances or other sources such as pensions.

DeLorenzo said he had made numerous loans, both to and from his corporations during this period. He stated that there are notes and documents supporting each loan which he had made or which he had received. He further stated that the accounting system for Greatfield Corporation is handled by the bookkeeper. DeLorenzo signed all the checks personally. The head of the bookkeeping department then was Barbara Keats, who now works for English & Calahad. DeLorenzo stated, on occasion he may have personally endorsed checks received by Greatfield, but these checks, gross receipts of Greatfield, always went into the corporate bank account. "At no time did I ever deposit these checks into my personal account." Any amount draws, salaries, or loans from the corporation would be by check, and there would be a loan document.

"I never make large expenditures in currency. Normally the largest amount of currency I have is $200 to $300 at one time. I have no hoard or pot of money." His smile had little warmth. "I do have another personal bank account which is for my airplane. On occasion I have paid some of the employees of Greatfield out of this account."

The special agents touched upon several more items and made an appointment with Michael for September 23. Michael promised that he would obtain copies of his tax returns, his bank statements and canceled checks, the loan account, and documents showing his liabilities to the corporations and his relatives.

Thus, by September, DeLorenzo knew full well that the FBI was conducting an investigation. He had been advised of his constitutional rights and the function of a special agent at the onset of his initial interview and at the onset of the subsequent interview. Michael DeLorenzo indicated he understood his rights.

During the initial interview in DeLorenzo's private office, the special agents noted a large green book entitled *Tax Fraud* on the shelf behind his desk.

According to the FBI records, no information regarding the personal history of Michael DeLorenzo was obtained from family members or third party documents. However, they were able to deduce some information:

They believed DeLorenzo was born in Haverville, Texas, forty-eight years before. His father's name is unknown. His mother's name is Frances DeLorenzo. He graduated from Normandy High School in Texas, joined the Navy, then briefly resided in Sacramento, California.

He married Anna Lee Corda, a/k/a Anna Morgan Corda in Sacramento, and had four children by this marriage.

DeLorenzo also had a daughter, Maria DeLorenzo, born the previous year, as a result of his relationship with Jennifer Surel, his ex-secretary and paramour.

Various documents and letters, submitted by DeLorenzo, indicate he graduated from college with a major in accounting and a graduate major in marketing. His graduate education allegedly included management courses at Wharton and an MBA from the University of Chicago. However, investigation did not prove this. DeLorenzo did attend some night classes at the University of Texas in Austin while selling insurance full-time, but he did not graduate from college.

DeLorenzo's family moved from Sacramento to Portland, Oregon after DeLorenzo had suffered a substantial period of unemployment which resulted in declaration of bankruptcy. DeLorenzo's training at Wharton occurred after this move, apparently consisting of several weeks of specialized training through a firm by which he was employed.

DeLorenzo is a voracious reader of business, legal, and tax literature and he is highly intelligent.

During one period ending seven years before, DeLorenzo held several jobs, most of which lasted less than a year. Between these jobs he was unemployed for extended periods. He attempted to start a business, "The Medical Services Bureau," working out of his residence, without success. Throughout this time his wife Anna worked to provide support for the family.

DeLorenzo found employment with the Starns and Hamms Company which is in the business of constructing, managing and leasing business parks. DeLorenzo was very successful and became the number one leasing agent of S & H.

While employed at S & H, DeLorenzo and Clifford Sabol, who was employed at Starns and Hamms as a design architect, put together a major lease package between the S & H Company and American Wholesale Grocery Company. As a result of this experience, DeLorenzo, Sabol, and a third party, Dan Allman, independently negotiated a contract with Cooker Foods Corporation to finance, design, construct and lease a frozen foods warehouse for $1.4 million. The business vehicle used for this project was a corporation, which was an investment club owned by Sabol and others, known as Liberty Enterprises, Inc. The voting stock of this company was divided one-third to each of the new partners.

DeLorenzo quit the Starns and Hamms Company to become president of Liberty Enterprises, Inc. with offices located in Portland, Oregon. Sabol also quit S & H and became the chief architect of the new firm.

DeLorenzo was the principal or sole stockholder of Liberty Enterprises and a series of corporations, moving from one to the next, essentially without change of assets, personnel, or facilities, as problems occurred with minority stockholders, bonding companies, banks, or creditors which infringed on DeLorenzo's operation of the predecessor company.

Liberty Enterprises, Inc. and Greatfield are now operated by Reems Insurance Company in an effort to reduce bonding losses, though DeLorenzo remains the stockholder. DeLorenzo Corporation is now dormant.

Numerous witnesses interviewed during the course of the investigation indicated DeLorenzo as a lavish spender. DeLorenzo so frequently entertained employees at the Thunderbird Hotel using company credit cards, it became known as the "Clubhouse" by company employees.

DeLorenzo and his family reside in an expensive waterfront home and drive company owned cars almost exclusively. Company records indicate DeLorenzo frequently flew Jennifer Surel, friends, and family members about the country in his airplane (for example to Seattle for dinner or to Mexico for a vacation). The aircraft used was a twin-engine turbo prop model, designed for business use and expensive to operate. The corporate pilot was always used on these occasions.

Company records show DeLorenzo frequently flew to Brownsville, Texas, where his mother and other friends lived, or to Reno or Las Vegas where he wrote company checks to pay for his entertainment. DeLorenzo purchased, used, and maintained at his residence's dock, several boats, both power cruisers and sail. He sent his wife and her parents on a Bermuda vacation.

DeLorenzo appeared to be in good health when interviewed. However, members of his family say he occasionally suffers from spells of acute depression, and that he has used amphetamines or other drugs during these spells.

DeLorenzo frequently referred to sophisticated tax concepts regarding his corporations in correspondence to third parties, demonstrating his knowledge of Federal Income Taxes. Exhibit 25 is a series of eleven letters authored by DeLorenzo during a two year period. These letters demonstrate the fact that Michael DeLorenzo consistently concerned himself with, and was aware of, the requirements and effects of Federal and local tax laws.

◆

When Anna and their children were informed of the FBI investigation into the "criminal aspects" of DeLorenzo's business affairs, an immediate polarization within the family took place. Overnight the children assumed positions of defense supporting Anna both emotionally and legally. Operating as corporate stockholders they had a brief meeting where they stripped Michael of his power in the company and prepared to defend themselves. Anna filed for a divorce.

Meanwhile, the FBI was unrelenting in its thoroughness, questioning Michael time after time. Michael was not known for either patience or tolerance of insubordination. The gauntlet had been thrown.

*O*n March 4 of that same year, officials of Western National Bank informed the United States Department of Justice of an apparent violation of title 18, Section 1014, United States code, by its customer Michael DeLorenzo, President of Greatfield Corporation and Liberty Enterprises, Incorporated. Bank officials advised that DeLorenzo, a customer for three years of the Portland branch of the Western National Bank had a satisfactory borrowing record with the bank until last year. During this time, DeLorenzo's companies had several construction expense liens, some of which were repaid within several days totaling as high as $500,000 and in connection therewith they had him furnish banking officials with an unaudited financial statement.

When pressed by banking officials to supply an audited financial statement concerning these companies in connection with the borrowing, DeLorenzo, on November 25, provided financial statements that purported to be audited and bearing the opinion of the National Certified Public Accounting Firm of Miles Henderson & Company. At that time, the amount of money outstanding as a loan to Greatfield and Liberty Enterprises totaled $200,000 and an additional $200,000 was borrowed on November 25 and another $200,000 on December 2. The current outstanding balance with accumulated interest due to the bank of Greatfield-Liberty Enterprises is $615,561.

The companies are currently in financial difficulties and the operations of these businesses have been taken over by the bonding company, Reems Insurance Group, and DeLorenzo was currently employed by the bonding Company in an advisory capacity.

Bank officials advised that they have been notified by the Certified Public Accounting Firm of Miles Henderson & Company that the audited financial statements of these companies, dated December 31, and purportedly signed by Miles Henderson & Company were not prepared by that accounting firm and the signature of Miles Henderson & Company of the financial statements is a forgery.

This matter was discussed with the United States Attorney's Office, which advised that the State Attorney would consider prosecution for violation of Title 18, Section 1014, following an appropriate investigation.

The scope of this investigation included examination of bank records, discussion with the bonding company, the Certified Public Accounting Firm of Miles Henderson & Company, and interview of subject, Michael DeLorenzo, concerning these financial statements.

Later in March, Greatfield Corporation received notification from the Miles Henderson & Company that a meeting had taken place in the offices of Reems Insurance Corporation. Reems Corporation and legal counsel representing Reems Corporation were present. Miles Henderson was shown copies of financial statements of Greatfield Corporation and Liberty Enterprises, Inc. together with reports purported to have been prepared and signed by Miles Henderson & Co. At that time they stated:

> We advise you that such financial statements and reports were not prepared or issued by us or signed by any representative of our firm. These documents are forgeries and Miles Henderson & Co. has not authorized their preparation or distribution.
>
> Further we state that our firm has never issued an audit report nor performed an examination of the financial statements of these companies in accordance with generally accepted auditing procedures, and therefore, we would not have been in

any position to render any opinion on such financial statements.

We are sending copies of this letter to those organizations and individuals who, to the best of our knowledge, have received copies of such financial statements and reports. The organizations are: Western Bank, Reems Insurance, English & Calahad, and Samuel Bremman, Attorney. Any other individuals or organizations to whom copies of these reports may have been delivered should be informed that they cannot place any reliance upon them or upon the opinion therein purportedly expressed by us and that they are forged documents. Further, if you have any additional copies of this report in your possession they should be destroyed and no copies should be distributed to any other person.

Miles Henderson & Company is reporting this matter to the appropriate prosecuting authorities to determine whether criminal action should be taken against the responsible parties.

Michael DeLorenzo was no stranger to litigation. He seemed to need turmoil in his life to feel alive. However, he was accustomed to having the whip in his hand. He knew the discovery of this forgery was going to wreak havoc upon his financial dealings. The procurement of large loans from Western Bank was the lifeblood for the growth and prosperity of his companies. Slight of hand was not going to mask what he had done.

As in so many times in the past, when he was faced with a downturn in fortune, Michael began to slip into a deep depression. Rumors abounded that he fought the moods with amphetamines and alcohol.

In the early fall, Arthur C. Blacker, assistant vice president and manager, Portland Office, Western National Bank, advised as follows:

Three years ago, President of Liberty Enterprises, Inc., came to the Western Bank, which, at that time, was known as the

Portland Bank of Commerce, at which time he opened a checking account and borrowed a nominal amount of money. At that time DeLorenzo was only associated with Liberty Enterprises, Inc.; however, he later formed the Greatfield Corporation of which he is also president.

Since the inception of the account, the bank enjoyed a good relationship with DeLorenzo and his companies and the account was handled satisfactorily, loans were repaid as agreed, including one loan that totaled $500,000. This good relationship occurred up until the fall of this year.

The difficulties with this account arose in September at which time, within a two week period, DeLorenzo borrowed sums of money totaling $600,000 still currently outstanding on the books.

The purpose of these loans was to provide money for construction costs for projects being built by Greatfield in the state of Washington.

During the last two years, Greatfield and Liberty Enterprises had outstanding loans with Western Bank which were being paid as agreed. His bank had previously received interim financial statements in July, for both Greatfield and Liberty Enterprises and inasmuch as this account was a commercial account, formal loan applications were not made but the companies merely produced their financial statements. Blacker stated that he made repeated requests for audited financial statements prepared by a Certified Public Accounting firm from DeLorenzo, who advised him on several occasions that he would bring them in as soon as they were received. DeLorenzo, however, in mid-May provided the bank with a draft of an earlier financial statement in worksheet form from the Certified Public Accounting firm of Miles Henderson & Company. Later, Blacker, in comparing these statements to the year end statement received October 1 of this year, said it was purportedly signed by the accounting firm of Miles Henderson & Company, and appeared to be substantially the same statement.

In October DeLorenzo hired a Certified Public Accountant by the name of Steven Kohler, whose duties were to provide financial statements of these companies to Reems Bank. Blacker was unsure, however, if Kohler prepared the statements that were later submitted to the bank, or whether or not he is still employed by DeLorenzo.

Blacker stated he finally received the audited financial statements which were allegedly prepared by Miles Henderson & Company from Mrs. Michael DeLorenzo on October 30. He specifically recalled that she brought them into the bank. "I noticed her, as she seldom came in and had nothing whatsoever to do with the business."

A review of the Liability Ledger for loan advances and payments received revealed loans and payments to Michael DeLorenzo and Greatfield Corporation/Liberty Enterprises, Inc.

Attached to the worksheet draft of the December 31 financial statements purportedly prepared by Miles Henderson & Company, was a letter directed to Michael DeLorenzo from Miles Henderson advising that the draft form was incomplete and requested that it not be shown to anyone. This letter was signed by Gerald Green of Miles Henderson & Company.

Blacker went on to state that the Greatfield balance sheet which was submitted by Miles Henderson & Company as of November 30, showed an asset represented by 2,395 shares of Travelers Hartford cumulative stock totaling $137,114 as an asset and he recalls asking DeLorenzo for this stock as collateral when his business checks started bouncing and the accounts were in an overdraft position. DeLorenzo informed him that the stock was in a safety deposit box at Western Bank and he would come in and take it out and furnish it to the bank as collateral. When DeLorenzo later came in with Reems representative Samuel Bremman and opened the safety deposit box, it contained no Travelers Hartford stock. Blacker stated, "I'm not sure whether or not this asset ever existed because I was not present when this safety deposit box was opened. However, I do know at the time it was opened that other stock and assets were removed from the box."

*T*he more I found out about the complicated lives of Michael DeLorenzo, the more disgusted I became. How he managed to keep them separated and unaware as long as he did amazed me. There was, among some papers I located, an account by Michael and Anna's daughter, Lucia, which documented his careful lies when loose ends began to unravel.

In it, she told about a woman named Janet Cleager calling her. Cleager asked a lot of questions and finally, though she hated to, told Lucia some news. She went to a "coffee" at a neighbor's home. There she met a woman with a little child named Maria running about. The woman was named Jennifer Surel. This woman was showing the little girl's Catholic christening pictures, taken of the family with the baby.

Janet recognized Michael, and Jennifer said that was Michael DeLorenzo, the child's father. Janet was flabbergasted and asked if she knew he was married. Jennifer said yes, but that he was getting a divorce and his wife knew all about it.

The child was apparently born at County Medical Center. Jennifer went into the hospital under the name of Mrs. Michael DeLorenzo. Finally, Michael told Jennifer he was divorcing Anna. He did not mention, however, that his first wife had left him, and instead, led her to believe the opposite.

Jennifer was investigated by the IRS and she thought that it was because she hadn't filed any tax returns. They told her it was because they were investigating Michael and they knew about their situation and were checking out pleasure trips written off for business purposes.

Not long afterward, Michael took Jennifer over to their house and showed her that Anna's clothes were gone.

One month later, Michael took Anna on a trip to Mexico. When Jennifer learned of it, she was furious. She accused Michael of lying to her all along about his divorce. She was struggling to feed her family and he was off playing the big shot. She bought a round trip ticket to Mexico and found him at his hotel. At the hotel she told him off and then flew home.

◆

No one can be in the vicinity of a person whose life is coming apart without being affected. Wife, lover, child, friend, coworker, minister, subordinate, even attorneys are ultimately touched in a negative way. Living with Michael DeLorenzo had been difficult for years for Anna and the children. With the added stress of a criminal investigation, Anna could no longer be persuaded or coerced into remaining. She consulted a mental health counselor and an attorney.

Six months after Michael's first FBI interview, he was under oath in deposition for a divorce action. Many of the questions were an unpleasant reenactment of the special agents' points of interest. Michael's business and banking practices were under the scrutiny of scores of attorneys, both civil and criminal. Events moved at an accelerated pace from that time on. Michael's attempted suicide was explained away as an inadvertent overdose of sleeping pills. Anna left her job out of fear for her safety and she missed a confrontation with Michael when he showed up at Joint Health Medical only moments after she was taken to a safe house for abused women. His surrender of a hand gun to the Portland Police Department was brushed aside by the sanitized words of his attorney, "references to a gun and to suicide should not have been made a matter of public record."

In February, another affidavit was filed by Anna DeLorenzo. She was concerned for the safety of both herself and her daughter. Both of them went into hiding. She stated, "My husband is very angry with me and has threatened reprisal on myself and my children, who have come to my aid in this matter."

Michael had threatened their other daughter, saying that he might put a bullet through her head and meet others attempting to aid her with a "rain of bullets." Because of past threats, brandishing of a gun, and other acts of violence against the family, these threats were taken very seriously. Anna was also frightened by these threats and with the approval of a Joint Health psychologist, she moved. Her daughter helped her to move and to know exactly what Anna took with her. They had only about an hour before they expected Michael to come home from Joint Health Hospital after an overdose of drugs. Due to what the psychologist described as his "dangerous condition to himself and to others," they took very little in order not to enrage him.

The court granted a protection order, but when Anna tried to return to her home to get her belongings, Michael was there. Anna's later affidavit states, "Mr. DeLorenzo then commenced to become abusive and interfered with her attempt to obtain the few pieces of furniture the court allowed her to receive. Mr. DeLorenzo grabbed four briefcases full of documents and a box full of records and rushed them out to the trunk of the Maverick car he had in the driveway. He also grabbed a file hidden behind a bookcase."

The divorce action was proceeding at the same time as the IRS investigation. Anna went to the Federal Building in Portland to meet with special agents. Anna said that they seemed to know everything that had happened in their lives. They told her that there was investigation going on of Michael DeLorenzo's tax liability. It was not an audit but an all-encompassing coverage of Michael's corporations, and all his financial activities as best as could be determined. It had been underway for some time and they had accumulated a substantial amount of information and testimony. They intended to talk to the family as well.

Because the family had joined forces to protect Anna and themselves from Michael and the repercussions of his illegal actions, Michael treated them all as enemies. His threats were far ranging and taken seriously by each one of them.

The FBI had enough evidence by then to arrest Michael DeLorenzo for three years of income tax evasion as well as criminal bank fraud, and diverting corporate funds. Wherever Michael went he was followed by agents since there was a lot of money still unaccounted for.

At this time, Michael DeLorenzo was living at Jennifer's home. While he was sleeping one night, she borrowed his Cadillac to get some groceries. When she opened the trunk of his car to load the groceries, she found a large envelope along with a bundle of records. She looked in the envelope and found that it contained two bundles of currency. It was such a shock, Jennifer became hysterical. Crying, she fanned the bundles, which were secured with rubber bands. One bundle, about an inch thick, was all one hundred dollar bills. The second bundle was about one-half inch thick and was composed of twenty dollar bills. Jennifer put the money back in the envelope and placed it back in the trunk where she found it. The following Friday, DeLorenzo took her to a restaurant for dinner. Jennifer asked about the money that she had found and Michael asked her, "Do you want to know how much money is in the bundles?"

Jennifer said, "Yes."

"They contain $73,000."

"Why do you have it?"

"I just removed the money from the bank, and I'm going to make a payment to Reems Insurance Company."

Later, when DeLorenzo went to the office of Jennifer's attorney to give a deposition, he was asked about the money. DeLorenzo then stated the money was given to him by his family to purchase stock in his new company, Able Management Associates.

Subsequently, DeLorenzo said, "I hid the money in the DeLorenzo residence. The only person who knew where it was located was my wife, Anna, but after Anna left I found the money missing and presumed she took it."

Michael must have believed Jennifer wouldn't testify against him if they were married. While FBI officers continued their surveillance, he married her, then dined and danced at a posh hotel late into the evening, toasting his bride with champagne. The officers were the first ones to know that Michael DeLorenzo paid the hotel bill with a check written on a closed joint checking account he had shared with his ex-wife Anna.

Jennifer came across some pills that Michael had hidden. It alarmed her because Michael was drinking a lot and taking a variety of uppers and downers. On impulse, she threw the pills outside. When Michael discovered what she had done, he shoved her down the hall into her bedroom. He hit her hard and she slammed into the closet door and then fell backwards on to the bed. He grabbed her by the wrists and began shaking her back and forth. He pinned her wrists together with his left hand and hit her again and again.

He was yelling, "You nosy bitch. What I do is none of your business. If you ever touch anything of mine again, you'll live to regret it." Finally he released her.

Jennifer just lay there, totally shaken. After a long cry she convinced herself his violence was a result of the medication and the enormous stress he had been under because of the FBI investigation. She didn't recognize it as the danger signal it really was. However, she went away for several days to rest and think.

Michael called and apologized, begging her to return saying he realized how much he loved her and Maria, and how much he needed them both. Jennifer wanted to believe him. "I didn't want to see the ugly truth," Jennifer said quietly. "—That he would never change."

Early the next day she met Michael in the parking lot at the Swedish Hall in Portland and let him take Maria with him for a visit. He said he'd bring Maria home that night. He didn't. Jennifer called Michael's number constantly. Finally Michael answered. She was crying so much she could hardly speak.

"Where is Maria?" she begged.

Michael started laughing and said, "You're not going to see her again."

"He kept up his threats until I was hysterical," said Jennifer. "Finally, Michael said quietly, 'If you don't like it why don't you kill yourself? My gun is under your bed.' Then he hung up. I dialed and re-dialed the telephone. There was no answer. I was frantic. I searched my mind wildly for someone who might be able to help me.

"I enlisted the help of Kurt Fellini, an old friend who was retired from law enforcement. Together we canvassed the neighborhoods of people who knew Michael. After a long and difficult search we located Maria at the home of one of Michael's friends. With the protection of a Portland Police Officer, I snatched Maria from their backyard."

Despite all this, Jennifer took him back. Soon the FBI arrested him. Several agents came to the house and asked Jennifer to wait outside while they put the cuffs on Michael. She was shocked. In spite of the fact that they had questioned Jennifer regarding some of Michael's activities, he had always been able to explain her doubts away. It took them less than three minutes to take him away. After the trial in which Michael was found guilty, he was sent to the state penitentiary.

For eighteen months Jennifer visited Michael in jail once a week. By the end of the first year she was occasionally told by Michael not to visit him so that his attorney could come. Once when he miscommunicated she arrived to find not his attorney but Simon Kiel, the man Michael claimed had embezzled funds from the Boardman job and bragged of not having paid income tax for years. Jennifer received an icy welcome.

For each visit Jennifer took the ferry to the jail, and Maria, only two years old, came with her. During that period, Jennifer was injured in an automobile accident. After the accident she suffered from headaches as well as mysterious stomach cramps whenever visiting day approached. Her doctor insisted she wear a neck brace but had no diagnosis for the stomach ailment other than attributing it to the continuous stress with which she lived.

Whenever Jennifer came to visit, Michael castigated her for wearing the brace and finally forbade her to wear it at all. The next time she came, she brought a note to Michael from her doctor explaining that she needed the device and asking for his understanding. Michael relented, apparently appeased by the deference. However, his lack of sympathy was the turning point. She finally realized how little regard he had for her. She began to think of divorcing Michael and that led to feelings of intense guilt.

She oscillated, and at times some of her old love for him would come flooding back. She had an enormous emotional investment in the relationship. She tended to dwell on the good old times, the trips and the exciting things they had done. But more and more often she had to face the realization that only when she totally surrendered to his irrational demands and control could peace be maintained.

Deciding to leave him permanently was not a decision Jennifer made lightly. Her first divorce had left her with unhealed scars and a deep guilt over not being able to hold sacred vows unbroken. The long hours of being alone had strengthened her ties to her Catholic faith. She was dealing with a lot of guilt and fighting the overwhelming need to maintain the relationship no matter how harmful it was. She hated the idea of failing again.

Michael may have sensed her withdrawal for he began telling her long stories of things that had happened to people who proved to be disloyal or crossed his friends in the Mafia. He often spoke kindly of his friend Lennie Magalio, even hinting that he wanted him to be Maria's God-father. Jennifer was grateful that Maria had already been baptized as a tiny infant. But the subtle threats were not lost on Jennifer. Across her mind the thought filtered, he'll destroy me if I try to leave.

The thing which plagued her most, however, was her sense of fair play. She could not bring herself to leave Michael when he was down. "I'll wait until he is out of prison, then I'll leave," she told herself. Michael's possessiveness had severely limited Jennifer's world and spending all her spare time visiting him in jail did so even more. It was a vicious cycle. The more dependent she became, the more willing she was to give in.

Michael was released to a halfway house, and after a required period of adjustment, they resumed living together. Jennifer didn't get home from work until late so Michael came and went as he pleased, offering no explanation.

◆

Not long after Michael's release from prison, Jennifer went to see her doctor. Because of lingering problems due to the automobile accident, she was scheduled for an E.E.G. test. They told her to arrange a ride home afterward. She asked Michael to take her to the appointment and bring her home. He agreed to do that.

At the test Jennifer was very frightened. "They inserted the needles, then wiggled them," she said, "They're electrically charged. When they increase the current you involuntarily shake."

The purpose of the test was to try and see if there was any nerve damage in her shoulder since she suffered periodical numbness since the accident.

Michael was supposed to pick her up after this test. It was in the early spring and still rather chilly. He didn't show up.

She telephoned Michael numerous times, but there was no answer. The doctors had to stop the test because Jennifer became so stressed. Finally Jennifer left and went to the bus stop. She was so upset she started crying and couldn't stop. All she could murmur was, "Where are you when I really need you? You're not working and there's no reason why you shouldn't have been here with me."

After that incident Jennifer stopped and looked at Michael searchingly. Not long afterward, Jennifer learned Michael was seeing Alicia.

She went on, "It was such a shock to my system doing that test. Maybe that was what I needed to evaluate my situation. I was still trying to recover from the shock of his indifference to my pain when I saw him with Alicia."

A short while later, Jennifer filed for a legal separation. Her relationship with Michael had deteriorated steadily since Michael's release from the halfway house. He didn't need her anymore to create the stable family home picture for the benefit of his parole board. Within three months of his release he took up with Alicia. He stopped coming home regularly. "He told me that he was traveling for Johnny, for whom he worked, or was with Magalio, and I was not supposed to ask questions of him," Jennifer said.

"Did he actually see Magalio, or do you know?" I queried.

"I don't know for a fact. I only know what he told me. I did see a letter he wrote to Magalio in Tucson," Jennifer said.

Jennifer filed for a restraining order against Michael. On the fourth of July, a neighbor called her and said that Michael was parked across the street in a dark area watching the house. "She warned me to be careful. She knew there was a restraining order and he was in violation of it."

Later, Michael got a month's visitation with Maria granted by the court. Jennifer had no funds for a big court battle, but she did have temporary custody of Maria. The only stipulation was that Jennifer not take her out of the state. They gave Michael his month's visitation starting August first. Because of Michael's threats, Jennifer tried to block it every way she could.

"Michael had told me before, that once he had control, I'd never see Maria again. I was scared. As August neared, I became more anxious. He would have a whole month to find a place to hide her. I called my friend, Rich Stevens. He suggested that I get the hell out and hide. The closer the time came to Michael taking Maria, the more unclear my thinking became. Finally, I called Pam

Clancy, an old friend from college who lived out of state. Pam said, 'Come to Denver. You can stay with us until you get settled.'" Jennifer called up the airport and made a reservation under an assumed name. Her neighbor Mrs. Moore, Rich, and her mother helped pack Jennifer's belongings. Within two days, Maria and Jennifer were gone.

They each took only two suitcases so as not to arouse suspicion. The rest went into storage. Rich put her things in two different storage lockers. He was a private detective and he filled out the paperwork under one of his aliases. After Jennifer paid for the plane tickets she had only twenty dollars left.

At the airport, Jennifer kept looking around, afraid all the time that Michael might have seen her moving or figured something out. She and Maria got on the plane and a few hours later they were in Denver. Pam picked them up and took them to her home.

By Halloween they had moved into their own apartment. Jennifer found a wonderful preschool and a good job with the Denver Child-Aid Department. She felt peaceful for the first time in years.

Chapter Nine

Alicia's Story

The woman with whom Jennifer had seen Michael was Alicia
McNeal. She was a gentle person with short black hair, green eyes,
and attractive. She had one son whom she adored and because her
husband had recently died, she was also well off.

She was introduced to Michael through his friend at the time,
Alex Solimine. One of Alex's coworkers, Ellen Malloy, who knew
Alicia well, was dating Alex. One night, while the three of them
were out together, Alex introduced Alicia to Michael DeLorenzo,
who Solimine said was in the process of getting a divorce.

Within a week Michael called and asked Alicia to dinner. On
their first date Michael and Alicia hit it off. They began to see each
other regularly after that. Since Alicia was a person with high
moral standards she never had Michael stay at her home because of
her young son, nor did she stay in his.

Nevertheless they became close, spending long evenings and
weekends talking about the past and future.

During this time, Michael confessed to Alicia his earlier
problems with the IRS and his stay in prison. He called it a fiasco.
He was the contractor on some building which went belly up and
because of all the problems occupying him he hadn't filed personal
income taxes for two years. The IRS came in and audited him and
that's what the charges were.

Not only did Michael talk about his business problems, but
he also discussed his daughter Maria—how much he loved her and
how her mother's pregnancy had destroyed his first marriage.

According to Michael, Maria's mother, Jennifer was a horrid person who had an awful temper and a tendency for hysterics, fainting, and lying. To confirm his appraisal of Jennifer, Michael had Dr. Ogdon Leeds, a friend of his, call Alicia and reaffirm not only Michael's words but add that Jennifer had heavy mental problems. Another of Michael's friends told her approximately the same things.

What made the greatest impression on Alicia, however, was Michael's concern about how his ex-wife was treating Maria.

When Jennifer took Maria from Portland, Michael's fears escalated. He searched everywhere for the child and hired detectives.

Since most of Michael's money was tied up in the divorce litigation, he begged Alicia to let him use some of hers. Alicia, who had been left life insurance, money market certificates, and a one-hundred-thousand dollar trust fund for her young son, agreed.

Not long afterward, Michael and Alicia married and moved to Franklin Island. They would live there almost five years.

When Michael announced that the detectives had found Jennifer and Maria in Denver, they both rejoiced. However, Michael said dejectedly, "It will cost a lot more money. I'll have to hire really good attorneys in Portland and Colorado to get her back."

Money flowed out quickly, but Alicia begrudged none of it. She could only imagine how horrible it would be for her and her son to go through a traumatic experience like the one Michael and Marie were suffering through now. If she were in that situation she would want someone to help her so she was very sympathetic.

They even eventually took Michael's ill mother to live with them until she had to be put into a nursing home.

After he and Alicia appeared in a Colorado court hearing, Michael was awarded custody based on the Oregon custody order. Afterward, Alicia went with him to get Maria.

For a while, as long as Alicia's money held out, things went along smoothly for them as a couple though Alicia could not stop the inevitable questions going through her mind.

Michael's business life went from one disaster to another. At one point they had to move to Michael's boat which they moored at a private marina for a year. They finally moved to another apartment in Portland. Shortly after this, Alicia's inner turmoil about Michael's and her life escalated. When she found out all her money was gone, and more law suits were filed against him, she broke down and had to be hospitalized. A few weeks later she returned to live with Michael. The marriage was over. Alicia finally walked out, taking Maria and Robert with her.

They went to Alicia's mother's house. However, in Alicia's nervous state it was all she could do to take care of her own child. She called Michael. "You have to pick up Maria," she said. "I'm an emotional wreck and I just can't take care of her." But there was a further reason: despite all Michael had done to her, Alicia still cared. She was worried about him and thought he needed Maria as a responsibility to keep him straight—to keep him from falling apart. Her spirit and her heart were broken. Moreover, she was frightened because Michael had always told her, "If I can't have you, no one can." Alicia filed for an Order of Protection.

A few weeks later she reluctantly filed for divorce. Though there were many problems and Michael had used a good deal of her money, she still had deep feelings for him.

She could hardly believe it a few weeks later when Alex Solimine telephoned. "Alicia," he said, "there's a problem."

"What's one more problem," she replied sarcastically. "I have a million."

She heard a sharp intake of breath. "Michael has remarried," he said quietly.

"But we're not divorced yet," Alicia protested.

"I know," Alex replied. "I know."

When Jennifer and I met again, something was on my mind. Unable to contain myself I asked, "Jennifer, how did Michael get custody of Maria?"

"It was months later when my attorney sent the papers to Oregon. That's how I learned Michael had divorced me. Because I fled, he was granted custody even though Maria was with me in Colorado. When the papers were served on Michael, he knew exactly where I was, because private detectives he had hired had located me soon after I got to Denver. But he kept spending Alicia's money, telling everyone he was using it to try to find me. It was untrue. Michael and Alicia came down to take Maria in November, but Michael had known where we were since March of that year."

"He used Alicia's money, supposedly looking for you," I said. "No wonder she was sucked in."

"He knew where I was," Jennifer insisted. "He sent several letters to me at my work address and also one to my sister-in-law's address. In one he threatened me, but said that Maria was happy with her new family." She handed a letter to me.

Ms. Jennifer DeLorenzo
1697 Grant Ave
Denver, CO 80215

RE: Attempts to locate Maria, Michael

Dear Jennifer:

As I told you in Colorado, DO NOT attempt to locate either Maria, myself, or other members of my family. Jennifer, I thought that you would have learned by now that you cannot win. Maria is very happy with her new family and has more than any little girl could wish for in new clothes, books, toys, and her very own television.

Jennifer, take my advice for once in your life and don't embarrass my friends or yourself again. No one, I repeat, no one, is going to help you. When will you realize this? I have seen to it that you will never get any information regarding Maria from anyone but me. You must follow my rules:

1. No attempts to locate us, or any members of my family.

2. You will not return to Oregon.

3. You must return my paintings, papers, and other possessions.

I care for Maria very deeply and will not have you attempting to upset her. Jennifer, you don't have a chance—give it up. I hope you realize that this is just for my concern for Maria's well being and safety and is in no way a threat to you or yours. I hope we can remain on good terms as we have our darling daughter to think of.

If not however, I am prepared to do what it takes, legally, to prevent your unauthorized contact. Just so that you know I am serious, remember that I could force you to pay child support, but as I told you in Colorado I have no intention to, as the amount was just punitive and I don't need it, nor does my family.

Maria does get your letters and cards and I speak well of her mother, so quit while you are ahead of the game.

Yours truly,
Michael DeLorenzo
Enclosed: Dissolution

She looked at me intently, thrusting a legal looking paper into my hand. "Please don't be angry," she pleaded. I took the paper and settled down to read it on my couch. Many of the words I had spoken to Jennifer nights before leapt at me from the paper. I felt uncomfortable and used. She hadn't told me she was going to use my statements for a legal document.

The statement outlined Michael's bigamous marriage and his attempt to swindle me. The past two years had been so difficult. Now I just wanted to forget. I felt angry and threatened knowing that once this statement was used in a courtroom, chances were pretty good that Michael would seek revenge.

Jennifer stayed far into the evening. She showed me photographs of Maria as a young child plus documents and press clippings that detailed Michael's legal battles. There were more than four, single spaced pages of court docket numbers, each representing an arrest and court appearance. Having them together was appropriate; it constituted their life together.

Jennifer's maternal pride and love for her daughter was apparent. She handed me a current photograph of Maria, now fourteen. The same blond hair and solemn eyes that I recollected stared back at me. Makeup and earrings helped transform the child I remembered into the pretty -teenager smiling for the camera, but the lackluster expression of her eyes bothered me. What were those eyes saying?

As Jennifer talked, I wondered what I should tell her about Maria and how Michael had made her confirm his falsehoods. Maria had been Michael's pawn, and he taught her to lie adroitly. Should I warn Jennifer or allow her the joy of having found her precious child? For the time being, I would keep silent.

As the evening wore on, Jennifer eventually told me about how Michael had kidnapped Maria. Once again, my sympathy for that poor child rose. Though I was desperately tired, I simply could not ask Jennifer to leave, not in her agitated state.

"He doesn't deny any of it. Of course, he has a new explanation every time for it all. Now he's trying to tell the court that he never knew where I was or he would have asked for child-support money."

"There's something that still bothers me. It's been seven years since you've seen Maria. Why did you wait so long?"

"When we were still married and Michael was in prison, he made friends with a man named Lennie Magalio. Lennie's father is a Mafia don in New York. Michael always bragged that they were cell mates. It's not true, but they were friends. Michael wrote to him after they got out. I saw the letters. That's not really what I meant to tell you." Jennifer, her emotions rising to the surface, stopped speaking, then began again.

"Right after I lost custody of Maria, I came out of the courthouse and found Michael waiting for me in the corridor. I was in shock over losing Maria. Alicia walked on ahead because Michael told her he wanted to speak to me. She didn't look back."

"Jennifer," I broke in, "the morning after the police arrested Michael, I had a telephone call from a woman who said she was his wife. Her name was Alicia. It was the only conversation I ever had with her. At first I thought she was trying to cause trouble. However, she asked me only one question. 'Were Michael and you married?' I just said yes. There were a few moments of silence, then she said, 'Oh my God.' Her obvious distress really bothered me after she hung up. Why did she react that way? Why?"

"Alicia's son hated Michael. He was about eight when his own father died. Michael came along promising his mom the world and never delivered. Worst of all, Michael took the boy's trust fund."

"How much?" I asked.

"A hundred thousand dollars."

"How could someone steal a trust fund? I thought they were protected."

"Alicia gave it to him."

"Damn," I said angrily.

"Oh, he promised to pay it back, but you know Michael," Jennifer said quietly. "That was the life insurance that had been set aside to pay for the boy's education."

"Where did it go? She and Michael were only married for six years."

"They bought a yacht" Jennifer said.

"I thought they sold her house in order to buy the boat."

"That was the first boat. Alicia's home was almost paid for. You have to have equity," Jennifer pointed out, "or there's no reason for selling it, you won't get any cash. Michael convinced her to sell that home and get one together that had no bad memories. Does that sound familiar?"

"I heard the same words when he wanted me to sell my home," I said, feeling disgusted.

Jennifer began speaking again. Her voice was soft, but the tone was desperate. "He was my only connection to Maria. Michael walked over and stood real close to me. I tried to plead without breaking down and begging because I knew from past experience it wouldn't work. He told me, 'I know that you're her mother and it shouldn't have come to this. I hope we can remain friends, that's best for Maria.' A small glimmer of hope must have shown in my eyes because that's when he told me there were conditions. I could never come back to the state of Oregon, never try to find them or contact any of his relatives. He said the $400 support payment was just punitive. When I asked to talk to my daughter, he ignored me and went on as if I hadn't spoken. He gave me a post office box where I could write him. I knew then he would never let me see her. I begged him to treat her nicely.

"He said, 'You know I'm serious. You've got to know you can't win. You're never going to win. If you don't follow my rules Jennifer... You remember my friend Lennie Magalio? Well, if you try anything, I'll see to it you suffer more than you've ever suffered before. But before you go, your other child is going to suffer first. When she is no longer with you then, and only then, will you realize that everything I've said is true.'"

I sat very still, staring at Jennifer, trying to absorb this monstrous story. "Did he give any indication of what type of violence he was planning?" I asked.

"No, but I'd heard him rant and rave in the past. He told me what he planned. They weren't just idle threats. Michael was especially vindictive toward one attorney who had helped Anna, his first wife. Michael told me he really hated the man and he planned to have the authorities find him in his car with his balls in his mouth. He was very graphic. Michael said he wouldn't do it himself. His hands would be clean. He'd be safe." Jennifer paused.

"When Michael was in the penitentiary he told me a story about one of the trustees in prison who was giving him a bad time. One week the authorities found the guard's car smashed into one of the cliffs near the prison. If you hear enough of these stories you believe. . . you believe."

"How much of that do you think might have been designed to intimidate you, that may not have been true?" I asked.

"I don't know. I pray I haven't spent all these years being afraid for nothing. First I waited for my kid to grow old enough to protect herself. Then I needed enough time to come up here and get established. I knew I had to find Michael before he learned that I had come back for Maria. I didn't know exactly what to expect, but felt my best chance was to make an entrance through a courtroom door. I believed if he found me first I might just end up dead. I've been very careful. But now I really must go to court with him and try to get back my child. Please say you'll testify and help me. You can find out things about him I can't. I can't defeat him without your help. With it, I know I can. Please." She pleaded, handing me a paper from her lawyer.

"Let me think about it, Jennifer. Just for tonight," I said quietly.

As we said goodbye I struggled for the right words to caution Jennifer, to comfort her, yet help keep her expectations in check. "It concerns me to see you so excited. Maria is no longer the innocent little five-year-old you said goodbye to in Colorado. Her father has had years," my voice failed me momentarily. "The things he told her about you, his manipulation. . ." I looked at Jennifer intently, I hoped somehow she'd understand without my saying more. Jennifer didn't answer me. She just looked away nodding her head, then repeated her plea, and said goodnight.

As I tossed and turned in my bed my decision kept going one way, then the other. Why should I subject myself to the pain of being involved in Michael's life again? Yet how could I not help another woman who had been hurt by him, perhaps even worse that I had?

Later, thoughts of Maria, the child I had liked so much, pinpricked me. With help, Maria could become the sensitive, loving person one glimpsed. Without it, she would be sacrificed to her traumatic past. I knew then I would have to try to help her and her mother. Whatever the personal cost, I couldn't live with myself if I just walked away.

The next morning I walked over to my desk and applied a stamp to the envelope bearing Attorney Craig Walters' Portland address. I took one last look at the declaration, then signed, sealed, and mailed it.

I had no more lingering doubts about Jennifer's truthfulness. Her words rang true. I had also suffered at Michael's hand. However, there was a lot I still didn't know about this man I had married. I knew there wasn't going to be a lot of laughter involved in learning the truth.

My visit with Jennifer and the subjects we discussed stayed with me like a shadow. In as much detail as I could, I wrote out a long history of my marriage to Michael and how I had learned he was a bigamist. As I reviewed it, I wished I could tell Jennifer more of what I knew and bring some reality to her expectations. As I went about my new job and activities, Jennifer was never far from my thoughts. I worried about her finding out how much Maria had changed. I knew Maria, even at age fourteen, was as difficult to fathom as her father, and I was still learning about the things he had carefully hidden from me.

A week after I mailed the history, Jennifer telephoned. "I know you want to hear about the preliminary court hearing," Jennifer began. "Craig told them you'd be testifying. I think Michael was surprised we had found you. His response was basically that his marriage to you was a mistake he realized immediately. He said you were only together two or three days and the marriage was never consummated."

"Three days?" I replied. "Try six months and as far as never being consummated, tell him to spare me the jokes!" My sarcasm didn't go unappreciated. Jennifer's laughter tumbled through the telephone line.

"I've been going through my boxes of court files and depositions trying to get ready for the custody trial. I have extra copies of almost everything. I thought you'd want to read them?" There was a slight question in her voice. Jennifer still wasn't sure of where she stood with me. Was she testing me? If so, why? What was she expecting?

"Definitely," I answered softly. "I need to see them in order to understand how I can help." Several days later three large packets arrived by mail. Inside were dozens of legal papers. The disclosures were shocking. There were trial transcripts, FBI reports, copies of depositions, and newspaper articles relating to Michael's criminal activities. Also enclosed were pages of numbers, listing the court docket cases Michael had been tried for: income tax evasion, corporate fraud, bank fraud, forgery, and theft of various types, plus eight social security numbers he was known to use. The number of crimes was depressing but I was not surprised.

When we talked, Jennifer told me Michael presented Gayle Higgins to the court as his wife. He had married her a month before my annulment and six weeks before his divorce from his third wife, Alicia McNeal DeLorenzo. It was not a valid marriage but the court was, as yet, unaware of that fact. Worse still, according to one court document in my possession, Michael had already borrowed thirty-six thousand dollars from Gayle. Somehow I had to alert her.

I decided to call my friend Bart. When Bart had seen Michael at the church service on Easter, Michael had been with a woman. According to Bart, Michael had been visibly shaken when he realized that Bart had seen him.

Bart and I had talked many times since then and I told him I badly wanted a way to warn the woman, but we didn't know her name. Now I knew. I didn't waste any time when Bart answered the phone. "Do you remember the woman Michael was with Easter Sunday? I've got her name. Now you can have the parish priest warn her."

A few days later Bart called back. "I went to the Father, but he says he can't do anything. There's no proof."

"Maybe I'll have better luck with the police," I said. I stuffed as many of the court papers in a briefcase as I could fit and took them to the Portland Police Department. I asked to see a detective.

Moments later I began explaining Michael DeLorenzo's background and activities. Bill Jensen, the officer, listened politely then asked what I wanted them to do. "Warn her," I replied in exasperation. "Take her these documents. Do something. He's not her husband. She needs to know that."

"We can't just walk up to someone's door and make that kind of an accusation," Jensen replied. "If we are wrong we could be sued."

"Well, if you won't do that, at least take these court papers and start a case file on him. He is a menace and victimizes women in your precinct."

The officer shook his head. "No, I can't." He stood up. I realized I had been dismissed.

Anger boiled up inside me, "Could I have your card?" Reluctantly he handed me one. "Detective Jensen, since you refuse to warn Gayle Higgins, I'm holding you personally responsible for whatever happens to her or her finances. The police are always complaining that there is not enough community involvement. Well, I'm here, and I'm involved. I have a ton of material that you won't even look at. Your lame excuse is the defense that you might put the city at risk of a law suit. I thought, as a detective, you might be a little more interested in Michael's criminal activities, just maybe you might want to look into them."

I put Detective Jensen's card into my purse and strode out. The farther from the precinct I got, the angrier I became. What in the hell is the matter with our justice system anyway? I stormed to the blustery night air. I sighed heavily. My only alternative was to find a way to warn Gayle myself. But would she believe me?

In my attempt to bring a warning to Gayle, I searched through more storage boxes for proof of Michael's past criminal activities. Inside one, I found a folder of letters. Just as I was about to quit I saw one Michael had written to me. Although it would not help Gayle, I realized its possible importance to Jennifer. Rushing to the telephone, I called her.

"Jennifer, I've found something I think your attorney would like to see. Are you going to be home tonight? If so, I'd like to drop by."

I reached Jennifer's apartment about 8:00 P.M. and rang the bell. Jennifer looked tired and worried as she let me in. Her hand shook as she reached for the letter in my hand. With a deep intake of breath she exclaimed, "What is this?" She scanned the letter and smiled for the first time. "This is. . . boy, Michael's had it now, the turkey," she said. Turning to me, she asked, "Where did you find this?"

"It was in my stuff, stuck away." I answered. "When I was looking for some documents to give to Gayle Higgins, I found the letter."

Jennifer began to read aloud. "I have a well defined value system. I've long lost my intensity for material things, I drive a classic Eldorado and a nearly new Audi. . ."

"That's the one that Michael stole," I interjected with amusement.

"He also stole the court file on it. My attorney has been trying to get a copy from his former attorney." Jennifer responded, then continued reading. "Last year I sold a nearly new Chris Craft, memories took the joy away. . ."

"Well, you know...," I said laughing, "memories of the bank repossessing it."

For the first time Jennifer's moodiness lifted. "Oh, I love it," she squealed merrily. "He never went to Wharton. He never went to the University of...." She paused for a moment looking impish. "Oh, I forgot, he took one night class."

"Stop reading Jennifer," I said still chuckling. "I'm going to get sick from laughing." I tried to assume a more serious pose. "Now, what does it say about his military career? That is one of the main reasons that I wanted Craig Walters to have it, because Michael was always lying about his military career." I grimaced.

"Navy: fifty-two months . . . emerged as a Lieutenant, J.G.," Jennifer looked at me in disbelief. "Even I know the truth about that. He was only in the navy fourteen months. During that time he petitioned three times to get out. He was a cook second class." With that, both Jennifer and I lost it completely. We couldn't stop laughing, the tears of minutes ago forgotten. "Thank you, Sofia. Not only for helping me with my goal, but for helping me remember there's a humorous side to all this. Even if it's hard. It means so much to me to have you at my side."

I drew her over to the large, flowered, overstuffed, sectional sofa that filled most of Jennifer's small living room. An hour into our conversation it was littered with stacks of documents, letters, photo albums, two precariously placed tea cups, and the largest cloth doll I'd ever seen. "I make dolls as a hobby and I could scarcely miss this one."

"Did you make it?" I asked. "Who is that?"

"Yes, it's Maria," she said softly.

"I've never seen anything quite like it," I replied. "How long ago did you make it?"

"Over a year after he took Maria. It was the following Christmas. I made it for myself and my daughter, Emily, to try and help us face the fact that Maria was really gone. It was my way of having Maria with us. I dressed the doll in Maria's favorite party dress, and sat it in a chair near the Christmas tree. It wasn't an altar. I just needed to have her there, even that little bit of her," Jennifer explained.

"I would have been inclined to sit around and hold or rock the doll. I find it painful to look at it, even now second hand," I said.

"I mourned her loss in my own way. I'd find myself in her room, not intending to go there. When it was unbearable I'd sleep in her bed, or touch her toys." Jennifer sighed deeply. "I had to be careful not to let myself break down completely because my other daughter was there. Even after the shock wore off I couldn't go into a toy store or through the children's section of a department store without crying. Surviving after Maria was taken was hard. Emily was supportive, though she was just a young girl herself.

"We had a hard time facing Christmas. We didn't want to be at home, so we went to a nice restaurant for dinner. It was something completely different from what we normally did. We enjoyed one another as much as we could. It was hard too, because Maria was only six and loved Christmas so much. I kept wondering how she was. I had no clue. I sent cards and packages but there was no way for me to know if she ever got them, or if she did, that she was told from whom they came. I kept thinking she must feel that I deserted her, that I didn't care because I couldn't come rescue her. I think that is the hardest part for me even now...all these years she probably thought I didn't care, that I had forgotten her." Jennifer's voice failed and she choked back her tears.

"She never forgot you, Jennifer. When she lived with me I asked her what her memories were. She walked through your home in her mind. She described the rooms, the furniture, and her sister. She had those memories. She held on to them."

I reassured Jennifer as best I could.

I didn't want to ask her questions that might make her hurt more. I wanted to put her at ease; so I began to talk about my own life. "I have my own beliefs about a person's rights, Jennifer. I was twelve when my father died. My mother never liked her in-laws, so when he was gone there was nothing to tie us to my dad's family. We were separated from that whole family, and it was an enormous group of cousins I had played with. Without them, only my mother's brother and parents remained. Then not only my father, but his family was gone. It was a great loss. The huge gatherings at holidays or summer reunions were gone. I resented that. It was stolen from me and those years can never be replaced. The relationships faded away and most of the relatives are strangers to me now. Once those bonds are severed in childhood it is difficult, maybe impossible to reconnect them. I have strong feelings about what Maria experienced, because I know what it feels like. And in a way, what my mother did is very much like what Michael did to Maria. Neither had the right to do that to their children, whatever their own feelings may have been."

Jennifer seemed to visibly relax, agreeing with my sentiments. I felt we could now turn back to the information I needed to know to help her.

"You never seem to talk much about your family. Has your mom been much of a help to you in all of this?" I asked.

Jennifer looked at me with solemn eyes. She sat still for a long time and then spoke slowly. "She tries, but she can't seem to understand. Perhaps it's because her life with my father was so different than mine and when he died, nothing else seemed to matter. When I tried to explain I had to try to get Maria back, she just shook her head no. But I can't leave my child with someone like him without trying with all my might to get her back."

I sat quietly for a moment trying to absorb what she had shared. "Have you made any new friends since you came here?" I asked.

"Not really. I have a few that I work with but we're not close. I do have my other child, but she's almost grown now. I haven't been close to a man for years. Would I want to bring a new person, a friend, into this mess? No," Jennifer said definitively answering her own question.

"I wasn't really focusing on that. I was more interested to see if you had some real support, people who are there for you when things get tough." I explained.

"The answer is no, I'm pretty much alone. I'm scared but I want to fight. My mother isn't, my sister isn't, Emily has always been there but she feels like the fight is hopeless. I have the feeling that you sort of feel that way too." She looked at me questioningly. I returned her gaze.

"It has never been my character to lie. Even white lies feel wrong to me. I have to tell you my own feelings, Jennifer," I said as gently as possible. "Maria needs a lot of counseling." I paused and then went on, "...to undo the years of Michael's influence. The things Michael has made her a party to are horrible. I understand why it has happened, but it's so difficult for a child to understand. I can empathize with her knowing about her father's lies and criminal ways and not turning away from him. But he has made her backup his lies. I think that while she is bright and sensitive underneath, she still desperately needs therapy. You taught her right from wrong. She needs to be away from his influence and to relearn those values." Again, I looked directly at Jennifer and was saddened by the pain I saw. "In my opinion, you should focus on getting Maria the help she needs and trying to begin a new relationship with her. That may be by living with you or that option may not be open now."

Jennifer broke in, "It's too late you mean?"

"Possibly," I said softly, "but don't think that far ahead. What is important is a new beginning. That is why I have decided to help you. Not only for your sake, but for Maria's."

"I was thinking," Jennifer said, as I picked up my coat and handbag, "about what you said earlier about your father dying. That's something we have in common. I'm now the same age as my dad was when he died. When I was in Colorado I used to think about death a lot. I had so few memories left of him it scared me. One of my greatest fears was that I would die before I found Maria again. I want Maria to know that she has not been forgotten. I took her to Colorado to save her and I lost her instead. But I want her to know I never stopped loving her, and I want her to understand the truth."

"That's a very good thing to fight for, Jennifer. Let's dedicate ourselves to it and win." I hugged her. "See you at the hearing."

She smiled at me as I left.

Slowly I adjusted to my involvement in Maria's custody suit. In the next week or so I sorted through my storage, locating items Maria had left behind. There were some photo albums and toys, and something I didn't expect to find—a notebook journal and some letters she had written, but never mailed. I set them aside for Jennifer and went to see her that Tuesday.

I purposely waited until rush hour would be over before setting out. Jennifer greeted me, "I don't know how to thank you for coming, Sofia, and more than that, for your help."

While we sat on the couch pouring over the photos in Maria's book, I said "Jennifer, I know this is going to be difficult for you but tell me if anything strikes you."

Jennifer's attention was focused on the album. She commented on people she knew, sometimes guessing who they might be. I could see how hungry Jennifer was for any news regarding her daughter and I shared as many anecdotes as I could recall. In time, as I began to probe her feelings, my questions turned to her case and in her passionate answers I began to see how deeply she hurt.

"Michael says vicious things about you," I said quietly. "How do you feel about them?"

"If there is one thing my attorney does not seem to understand," Jennifer said, "it's how devastating, to me personally, are these terrible, untrue things that Michael keeps saying and putting in print. In court hearings and at every opportunity, you wouldn't believe the names he calls me. He refers to me in the worst ways. It gives me the slimiest feeling. I can't stand it. I just want to scream. That is the one thing I want to fight strongly. Craig said not to worry about those allegations because they're untrue. He doesn't understand. It hurts me to the core."

"Michael understands it, and he's drilled that story into Maria. It's been a prime weapon, I said disgustedly.

Jennifer nodded. "I know. Before I read Michael's first pleading, Craig made me promise that I wouldn't bring those things up to Maria. His reasoning was that we have our whole lives ahead of us. He said, 'Regardless of what Michael does, one parent should do it right. . . We don't want Maria torn back and forth in her mind.'" Tears rose to her eyes.

"After I read Michael's statement I went home and wept. I was scared to death. What would happen to Maria's self-image if she believed that her mother was unfit or evil? It was so totally unfair to both of us. On my next visit with Maria I talked to her about it and she admitted her dad told her I was an unfit mother. Worse, I could see she believed him. I told her it wasn't true. 'Deep down inside you know that it isn't true, Maria. There are a lot of lies being told and it really makes me angry. I resent him for doing that.' She just looked at me and said, 'Well, the two of you know.' I said, 'No, you know too, deep down.'

"For a person to do that to a child is so vile. It's devastating." I said, biting my lip angrily. "But that's his character. Nothing is too base if it serves his purpose." I paused. "Jennifer," I said, my voice hardened, "It can be easily disproved. I seriously doubt someone who was an unfit mother would be working in a government environmental protection office. They run background checks," I replied. I smiled and she smiled in return.

Then the room became silent. Looking around I saw I wasn't the only saver. Jennifer had half a dozen open boxes in her living room. Half sorted piles of paper dotted the floor. Jennifer began to rummage through them.

She held one up. "I found this in one of my boxes. It's just a paper scroll, but I had it framed years ago when I was married to Michael. This poem hung on my wall. Sometimes when I would get mad at Michael for belittling or abusing me, I would read it. Michael always told me I didn't love him enough, that I qualified my love. Michael felt no matter what his problems were, if I had enough love for him, I wouldn't be down on him. He threw the responsibility for our relationship all in my lap."

Jennifer began to read aloud. "It is written by Emmet Fox. 'There is no difficulty that love will not conquer. No disease that love will not heal. No door that love will not open. No gulf that enough love will not bridge. No wall that enough love will not throw down.' That poem, as beautiful as it is, almost destroyed me. Every time I felt like admitting that my marriage was a failure, I would read that and think I need to try harder—that I can't give up."

"Not think that 'He has to try harder'?" I asked, probing her overdeveloped sense of responsibility.

"No. That I had to try harder," Jennifer emphasized.

I shook my head. "Hmmm. That brings something to mind concerning Michael's son. I tried to get him to take an interest in Maria when the police arrested Michael for fraud, and his bigamy problems were exposed. Other legal problems, such as theft and forgery were also coming to light. I felt Maria needed a home with her own family. Mike Jr.'s response was, 'I'll talk it over with my sisters and we'll decide.' I never heard back from him. I understand better now, after reading some of the legal papers from Mike's first divorce. One paper described an altercation where Michael wielded a gun and threatened his family. They went through hell during their parent's divorce. They must still be afraid of him.

"Mike Jr. told Craig, about a month or so ago, that he's had contact with his father, and helped him out financially at times. I don't know to what extent. As for Maria, he has never met her. When Craig asked him for an affidavit, Mike Jr. mentioned that Maria was fourteen years old. 'If she's that old, she can make up her own mind. How could it matter now?' Craig's response was, 'I know she's fourteen. It's how she got to that age that matters.'

"However, I don't blame Mike Jr. or the others. Michael has never cared what his kids went through, not any of them. The last Mother's Day that Michael and I were together, he promised he would take Emily, Marie, and me someplace to celebrate. Then, he said that he had to go out of town on business. He never came home. On Mother's Day a concerned neighbor called. She told me she watched Michael's car race away from my house. She knew we were having family problems and she was concerned for me. I looked outside. There was a small bag sitting on my back porch. In the sack was one loaf of bread and a small turkey. For days, that was all I had in the house to feed myself and two small children. He had taken with him all the money from my paycheck."

That story affected me deeply. I took a deep breath to regain my calm. It was something I already understood. Michael's only real feelings were for himself.

I decided to try a less emotional subject. "When you decided to come back to Portland, how did you select your attorney?" I asked, thinking this question was a lighter one. But this made Jennifer open up even more.

She rushed on. "It's an involved story. A friend of mine worked for a furniture company. She told me that they were looking for someone. It was a nine-to-five job with no required traveling. I'd be home on the weekends. It sounded great. I started working there a week and a half later.

"My girl friend, Sharon, told me she had either seen Alicia [Michael's wife], or heard some gossip about her. Alicia had been at the Credit Union where Sharon worked. Alicia opened a new account in her former married name 'McNeal.' This was the first indication that she and Michael had separated or maybe even divorced.

"With that bit of information I went down to the courthouse and looked up the papers. I found their divorce was not yet finalized. The papers didn't tell me where Michael and Maria were, but it did say where Alicia lived. I wanted, in the worst way, to call her to learn something about Maria, anything at this point, but I hesitated. I decided to have my friend call instead.

"Alicia told her she had no idea where they were. She asked if I was in town and she said that I was. He asked her where Maria went to school, and if there were any photographs we could have. She said she had no idea where Maria was and that she didn't care. She wasn't rude, but she offered no help at all.

"Afterward I hired a private detective named Lynda Mahon to help me. I saw an advertisement. Her office was located only a few blocks from my apartment building. I hoped, since she was a woman, she would take more of an interest in my case. She didn't find Michael but she did give me good advice. 'Hire an attorney first. When you find Maria you may have to move faster than you think. You may not have time to look around for a good attorney then. You'll have to interview several attorneys before you find one that you like, or that is qualified to take your case. You should also get in touch with Eileen Robbins at Childfind.'

"As soon as I got home I called. I couldn't get through right away. We finally got together informally at Burger King. We talked for hours. I cried like a baby, because I'd found a person who might be able to find Maria. That in itself was emotional, but she was also asking me questions that made me feel she cared. She said, 'You can't guess what the circumstances will be where Maria is living. You should be prepared to move quickly.' I told her how meager my finances were. She said, 'That will make it harder to find an attorney, but there are some who will work with you.' She gave me a list of attorneys who specialize in finding and recovering children. One of the names on that list was Craig Walters.

"When I called for an appointment his secretary screened the call. She asked for more details explaining, 'He chooses his clients carefully. He may, or may not decide to talk with you.' I felt my heart go down to my shoes. It was another dead end. I kind of mumbled that Eileen recommended him to me, and that I was trying to find my daughter. She said she'd have him call me back. Two hours went by before he called me.

"'Hi. This is Craig Walters. Tell me something about your case.' I was at the only phone where there was even a modicum of privacy. It was a tiny room we used for coffee breaks. No one was there, so I closed the door. He started with a string of questions. 'How long has it been since you've seen Maria? What steps have you taken to find her? Have you hired an attorney before? Do you have any idea where she might be? What legal steps have you taken to get her back?'

"Suddenly, reality hit me and I just started bawling. I couldn't talk at all, couldn't answer his questions. He was so nice. 'Don't worry about it, Jennifer. Meet me in my office tomorrow morning at nine. Meantime, cheer up. Don't worry, we'll find her. Bring all the legal papers you have no matter what they are.'"

"I'll bet you had a huge file," I said.

"Yes," she smiled. "I had a giant file box. Nothing was in binders. They were all loose. I planned to put them in order that night. Instead, I ended up in the hospital. There is a duct or something inside my intestine that twists when I am under stress. It's extremely painful. I was in the hospital from 1:00 A.M. until 5:00 A.M. I kept saying, 'You can't keep me here. I have an appointment to keep.' They tried to calm me down. The doctor gave me a glycerin shot. Finally, they released me. When I found Craig's office I discovered he was on the twenty-first floor. I walked into his office looking like the wreck of the Hesperous, carrying that big box of disorganized papers. I'd had absolutely no sleep and little confidence he would take the case. Craig came out to his waiting room. When he saw the box he offered to carry it for me.

"Once we were in his office, he began asking me questions. I'd dig in the box trying to find appropriate papers. While I was doing that, he was sizing me up. I told him frankly what kind of man Michael was. 'He manipulates people and uses all the delaying tactics he can find to drag out litigation. Many people give up because of the expense. I have never known Michael to pay an attorney. He just uses them until they either withdraw or he reneges on payment. That's why he doesn't care about the expense involved. I have precious little cash. I can't afford to stop and start on this. Once I start, I don't want to replace my attorney.'

"He gave me some forms to fill out to initiate a search for Maria. He also asked for a copy of my divorce papers. I didn't have a copy, so he asked if I remembered who Michael's attorney had been. I did and Craig called him. I could only hear one side of their conversation."

"Tell me about it, " I encouraged.

"Craig said, 'Hey Dick, this is Craig Walters. I have someone in my office. I need a copy of a decree from a case you handled. It'll help me a lot if you can remember something about it. Do you remember Michael DeLorenzo?'

"Craig said the attorney just went off the ceiling. 'Don't ever mention that name to me again,' he yelled. 'All flash and no cash! That guy is a real loser.'

"Then we contacted an ex-detective from the Portland Police. While Craig waited for the detective to come to the line, he said, 'This guy is good. I don't want you to get your hopes up too high since it's been seven years. It could take some time to find them. You realize that, don't you? I mean you have to be prepared for that because one can't ever predict these things.' I held my breath anyway.

"The detective answered. Again, I heard only one side of the conversation. 'Yeah, the mother is here in my office. No, she's not going to take off. She's here to stay and she wants to find her daughter. Can you take a look in the computer?' All of a sudden Craig started laughing. 'You've got to be kidding. You want to check that one more time to be sure? I don't want to say anything unless you're certain.' All this time he's chuckling.

"I said, 'What, what?' Craig held his hand over the receiver. 'I'm not going to tell you, though I'm dying to. You won't believe it.' My head started to buzz. Craig hung up the phone, turned and said, 'He's in jail.' Never had I been so happy to hear about someone else's misfortune." Jennifer stopped her tale as she burst into resounding peals of laughter. It was so infectious I found myself laughing as well.

At last I could ask, "What was he in jail for that time?"

Jennifer paused to think. "It was either forgery and credit card theft, or theft and fraud involving some rings. It was such a choice place to find him, such an affirmation for me. I felt it was a sign that everything was going to work out for me. I needed that so much."

I tried to say something so that she wouldn't count so much on a future which I thought had little chance of occurring. "Jennifer you need to stay calm. This is a very difficult case."

Jennifer rushed on, paying little attention. "'Okay,' Craig said, 'I require a thousand dollars retainer fee. In your case it should be more, but I'll let you make monthly payments. Your bill can never be more than two thousand dollars at any time.' Those became famous last words. I owe him over twenty thousand dollars now, and believe me, I have been paying regularly.

"Before my next appointment I got my Oregon State driver's license and Oregon plates. When I walked into Craig's office I had the plates in my hand. 'I know you didn't say anything to me Craig, but I saw the look on your face when you saw my Colorado license. I thought maybe I better go do this,' I said, showing the new license plates. The embarrassed little smile and twinkle in his eye told me I had guessed right.

"We went to court the next day to get a protection order and start proceedings. The commissioner took me completely off guard, he was so overbearing." Jennifer paused a moment looking at me. "He said, 'After seven years . . . where the hell were you? Nobody is going to . . . I'll give you this temporary order, but if you think anyone is going to make it permanent you're crazy.' Craig could see I was rattled. He leaned over and whispered to me, 'It's okay, don't worry about it. Some people are jerks.'

"That's terrible when a person in a position of authority chooses to abuse one who stands before him," I remonstrated.

Jennifer nodded. "I was not feeling too secure at this point. Craig said, 'You've got to trust me, Jennifer.' He walked me back to my car and told me, 'I'll be in touch with you in a few days.'"

"What was Michael doing during all this?" I asked.

"The first thing Michael did was go to Support Enforcement. He told them he wanted his thirty thousand dollars back support and gave them my address. That was the first volley he fired. He wanted to make sure that I'd have no money to fight with.

"The next day I went to court. I was going to try for custody of Maria because Michael was in jail. Before the hearing, I was shaking like a leaf. Craig told me he understood how afraid I was. He asked for my trust and promised I'd never be left alone with Michael. 'I'm here,' he said. 'Everything is going to be all right.'"

"That must have been a very difficult scene for you Jennifer. Was Maria there?" I asked.

"Maria was in court with Michael and Gayle. She was sitting between them. Maria kept sneaking peeks at us, smiling tiny smiles. She shouldn't have been there in court. She was supposed to be available to the court, but not actually in the courtroom.

"There were tables arranged in an L, slightly removed from one another. Maria, Michael, and Gayle were at the front. I was at a table and could see Maria. She'd smile at me, catch herself, look stoic. Then she'd smile again. I didn't want her to get in any trouble with her dad, but we couldn't help our silent communication.

"Gayle took the stand and testified to having a great marriage; she said Michael was always taking such wonderful care of them both. She added that he was responsible and thoughtful. Under cross examination, Craig asked Gayle when she and Michael married. You could tell Michael had coached her. She looked at Michael and explained that she had met Maria in September, loved her like a daughter, and that she and Michael married in February.

"Craig asked her if she realized that Michael and Alicia weren't divorced until April of that year. She said it wasn't true. She kept looking over at Michael as if for signals.

"Craig took a new tack. He asked Gayle if she thought Maria had the right to get to know her mother. That set off an argument.

"'I'm her mother,' Gayle said. Craig's voice rose. 'No, you're not. Jennifer is her mother. Do you know the difference?'

"'Well, I don't understand your question Mr. Walters. I'm her mother,' Gayle replied stiffly. Craig's temper exploded. 'Well, that's the point. You don't know the difference. That's exactly the point I'm trying to make!'

"Later, Craig told me, 'That is the one thing that really irks me. There is nothing wrong with being a stepmother or stepparent, but they are not the mother. Nothing makes me madder than someone denying that.' When Gayle went back to sit with Michael after her testimony, she grabbed his arm and shook it. I could tell she was mad," Jennifer said. "This was a definite red flag for her. She should have gone to the courthouse to look at those records."

"You're not finished with that chapter of your life," I said.

"I know," Jennifer replied softly. "The judge said that if the child was considered at all, it was best for all parties to try and get along. We should settle this as quickly as possible. We went into a small side room to make arrangements for visitation. As the judge was leaving, Michael started to make a loud statement, for the judge's benefit. As he began protesting, Gayle said, 'Oh just be quiet, Michael.' She was angry. Meanwhile, Maria was standing between them, next to Mr. Hadon, Michael's attorney.

"Hadon spoke up, 'Well, I don't know what the mother wants. She claims that this is her daughter, but she hasn't bothered looking for her for seven years. What does she want with her now? You call yourself a mother?' he said, glaring at me. Meanwhile, I was trying to get a phone number so I could call Maria. Hadon did what he could to degrade me in front of Maria.

"Finally, it was time to go. As we were leaving, Michael forced his way between Craig and me. He said, 'Just to show we mean you no harm, why don't you give your daughter a hug? We want you to be able to have a relationship with Maria.' Maria just stood there. The atmosphere was so charged. I did my best under the circumstances. I understood what Maria was up against. She was stiff as a board under her father's eyes. So, I put my arms around her and whispered in her ear. 'I love you honey, and believe me, I haven't forgotten you for a moment.' It should have been a private moment. Maria should have been allowed that moment alone. It was so traumatic. I can't forgive Michael for that. He just has to control everything.

"Later that afternoon I was sitting on a courthouse bench, reflecting on what had happened in court. I was still trying to reconcile seeing Maria as a teenager with the Maria I knew as a six-year-old. As I sat there, Craig looked over at me. 'Why do you have that strange smile on your face?' I was so overwhelmed with seeing my daughter again, all I could reply was, 'Isn't Maria beautiful? Isn't she just beautiful?'"

Chapter Thirteen
Poems of Darkness

*T*he preliminary hearing that day was the first big step in the family court dispute between Jennifer and Michael DeLorenzo. Jennifer was scared. I was not going to allow her to be alone in court with only her attorney as an ally. I told her I was going with her to lend some moral support.

Walking into the courtroom, the first person I saw was Michael. The intensity of my reaction at seeing Michael took me off guard. Being physically frightened was not something I'd expected. I was glad I saw him first, it gave me a few moments to gather my courage and present a confident face to Jennifer. She needed it, and so did I. If courage is lacking, there's nothing like bravado to get you through. I slipped quietly into the courtroom and seated myself beside Jennifer and her attorney.

Craig Walters had light brown hair and a pleasant looking face which seemed to connote an easy going personality. This air of ease was contradicted, however, by his deep brown eyes. In them there was an intensity of concentration which reminded me of Ralph Nader. Although we didn't speak, he seemed pleased that I was there. The proceedings were already underway. Michael's attorney, Byron Hadon, was speaking; Craig Walters was jotting notes. I squeezed Jennifer's hand. Her hands were icy. I rubbed them with mine and gave her a warm smile. She smiled back at me. I was glad I was there for her.

Michael's criminal record was discussed before the judge. I noticed that Gayle and Maria were not in court this time. After a time the judge took a short break. Michael stood up. He made a slight turn in order to speak to his lawyer, and caught sight of me. His shock at seeing me in court was written on his face.

Once again I was glad I had come. His look also told me that Gayle and Maria must be nearby. I knew the last person Michael would want them to meet was me.

Michael whispered to Mr. Hadon and left immediately. Jennifer had been watching me and we exchanged glances, hesitated a moment, then burst into laughter. It was a great moment to share, but a long period of waiting began afterwards which kept us both on edge until the session ended.

◆

During the next few weeks, I was cleaning out the basement and found a folder containing a number of faded, yellowed poems written in German which Michael had left behind. I mailed them to my stepfather. He had taught school in Germany on a Fulbright scholarship. German was his second language.

Weeks passed. My own financial distress continued and the hard work I needed to concentrate upon if I was to survive consumed me. Stress still kept waking me at 4:00 or 5:00 A.M. Christmas came and went. It was a miserable time that year with no money for gifts.

January didn't seem much better. I was doodling at work one Monday and drew a picture of flat terrain with two huge tornadoes in the background and large raindrops in the foreground. It wasn't hard to see the drawing symbolizing my life.

My car was dripping oil or some other fluid, and my home was in foreclosure. I tried not to obsess on either calamity. I was doing all I could to stay afloat. I prayed that something good would happen soon.

Luckily, it did. Some friends lent me a car to drive, while others made repairs on my home, and my stepdad sent me enough money to bring my house payments current. My life began improving in patches.

Unfortunately, there were still rough spots. Along with the check, my stepdad sent translations of Michael's poems:

Dear Sofia,

Below I will put the German and English titles of your clippings with a summary of the content.

Harte Herzen - Hard Hearts (poem). Tells how hard hearts cause misery to others, reflecting their own darkness.

Frohherbst - Early Autumn. Romantic naturalism—How fall gives us restful joy, but tells of the relentless ongoing march from spring to winter.

Welche Fiende Wir Furchten Mussen - What Enemies We Must Fear. The external enemies are not the ones to fear, but the enemies within us; our sins and passions. Written by Joseph F Smith, Mormon.

Die Goldene Hockzeit - The Golden Wedding (poem). Romantic—Tells of going from when we are young, through difficulties, and now to peaceful rest, together, in the bridal chamber of the grave.

I read the summary and wondered at the darkness it reflected.

Soon after that, Jennifer and I got our first break in the custody case. Jennifer was awarded limited visitation. Because I had been letting my work pile up while I helped Jennifer, I had to catch up and began working after hours and weekends. It was several weeks before Jennifer called me and said she had to see me again. When we met, she began immediately to talk of Maria.

"Our first visits were just wonderful. I was so excited just to be with her. The first visit Maria and I had away from Michael's home we spent going through boxes I had stored for years. They were filled with Maria's little clothes, toys and mementos. I had kept everything, whether it had any value or not. As I opened the boxes, Maria went through them separating the things she wanted to keep and have me store. Other items she chose to take with her. We donated what remained to Goodwill. As she looked at everything, she kept saying she couldn't believe I had saved all those things for her.

"I was in the kitchen preparing some lunch for us when she ran across some Avon perfume my mother had given her as a gift. I heard a squeal from the living room and then she was there beside me. She gave me a big kiss and a hug saying, 'Thank you for saving this. I used to smell this scent sometimes and I always associated it with you, but I didn't know the name of it. I sometimes dreamed of it. It nearly drove me crazy. Thank you so much.' She took it home with her.

"One day I took her to the office where I worked, to show her off, and also to see my friends Amy and Katy. They hadn't seen her since she was about five. I was so proud of her. She's grown up to be so pretty.

"Her memories of them were sketchy, but I'm certain she remembered Katy. She's unique, the type of person a child remembers. Katy used to have a pet chicken. In the evening when it was time to roost, the hen would come to Katy's sliding glass door and peck on the glass to be let in. She'd walk through the living room into the kitchen and fly up to a small child's chair that Judy has fastened to the kitchen wall. It was her roost and the only place she'd sleep. Maria remembered that chicken."

"That must have been fun but this is an emotional time for you. How are things going now?" I asked.

She shrugged. "Not very well. There has been so much interference by Michael and Gayle. When we first started having visits and it was time to take Maria home, she would beg for just a few more minutes. 'Please mommy, I won't tell, let me stay for just a little while longer.' As a consequence I was always a little late getting her back. Michael had put pressure on her though, and after a few weeks things began to change. First she'd miss a visit because something special was happening with one of her friends or there were other family plans she didn't want to miss. I tried to make as many allowances for her sake as possible, but I knew what was going on. Things have gone down hill steadily since then," Jennifer said sadly.

"Have you appealed to the court for help?" I asked.

"Yes, but there's only so much they can do. I have asked the court to respond to the recommendation of Berk County Court Services to order psychological evaluations of Maria, Michael, and myself. We're waiting for an answer from the court on that. Michael just ignores anything the judge orders, but he won't be able to evade an evaluation if it's directed. Sooner or later he'll have to comply or stand in contempt." Jennifer's despondency showed.

"Are you seeing Maria at all now?" I asked.

She shook her head.

"Jennifer, what happened?" I asked in dismay.

"When I first started seeing her, we had visits every Saturday between 10:00 A.M. and 6:00 P.M. Several times Michael tried to interfere but I just hung in there. Then Michael called me about 8:00 A.M. on Saturday and told me that a warrant had been issued for my arrest because I had not appeared at his attorney's office the day before to have my deposition taken. I knew that my attorney had taken care of that and no arrest warrant existed. Michael insisted that there was such a warrant and that I was likely to be arrested at any time and that he would not allow Maria to go with me because that would subject her to being present when I was arrested. I asked to speak to Maria, he told me she was not there, but that he would have her call me at 10:00 A.M. When I finished the conversation with him, I attempted to reach Maria at her home, unsuccessfully. I called my attorney at his home and he reassured me that no arrest warrant existed and advised me to attempt to have the visitation and not to be buffaloed.

"Since Michael told me that Maria would not be home I did not know what to expect, but I went to pick her up anyway. She was very surprised to see me. She obviously had been told that I was going to be arrested and that there would not be any visit that day. When I made it clear that I intended to exercise my visitation rights she got ready and we left. We had a good time.

"We continued having good visits after that, although it was difficult only having a few hours at a time. It was also clear that Maria was being pressured not to come with me and her attitude toward me was always much different when she was around her father and stepmother. You confirmed some of my worst fears about what had been going on in Maria's life while I was gone. It also helped me to understand some of Maria's actions better. The loyalty toward her father that he had instilled in her was obvious. It also became clear that, in spite of his denials in court, he had told her terrible stories about me.

"A month later Maria began to telephone and leave a series of excuses on my machine as to why she would not be seeing me on the scheduled Saturdays. Sometimes they were plans she made with girlfriends, other times no reason was given. One day she left a message on my answering machine saying, 'Jennifer, this is Maria, I'm not coming to your house on Saturday, um, and I don't care if you come to my house, I'm not going with you. Goodbye.' I called her the next day. Gayle answered and said Maria wasn't there. When I asked when she would be back Gayle told me 'later.' She had a negative answer no matter what my argument was and she finally said, 'Her Saturdays are taken up, and she's at an age where she can speak for herself. If she has defied the judge, that was her choice to make.'

"I didn't hear from Maria for almost ten days. When she finally called, we talked for a while. She kept insisting that she did not want to spend any more time with me. She could not or would not give me any reason why, just that she didn't want to and didn't have to. Eventually, the conversation going nowhere, I told her very clearly, several times, that I love her and will be there for her. I also told her I would pursue seeing her and that I would not just go away. It was clear to me that she had been influenced against me by her father. At one point in the conversation, she referred to Gayle as her mother and to me as her 'biological mother.' I finally ended the conversation and told her I'd talk to her later.

"A few days later we talked again. We had pleasant conversation for five or six minutes. I intentionally did not pursue any issues about our visits. She suddenly said her dad had just gotten home and she had to go. I told her I loved her and she said goodbye and hung up. I haven't seen or talked to her since then. Gayle called and said, 'This is Gayle, Maria's mom. Maria asked me to make the usual courtesy call. She will not be seeing you Saturday.'"

I shook my head sadly. "What can I say Jennifer? I feel so badly for what you've gone through. What are you going to do? How can I help you?" I asked.

"There's not much we can do," Jennifer said miserably.

"There's one thing," I replied emphatically. "You can go back to court." Listening to me she looked more nervous than ever. "You have to Jennifer," I said.

"You'll be there for me?" she asked plaintively.

I nodded and sighed heavily. "You can count on me. Let's get a court date."

Chapter Fourteen
Visitation Falters

Though months went by, I found that my financial worries were far from over. To ease the stress I began an exercise program. Several friends agreed to embark upon it with me. One, Nick Gillotti, who had been a survival expert in the army for four years, took us camping at Olympic National Park. Snow filled the mountain terrain and wind blew up at night. The air was fresh and brisk cold. In the daytime sun frosted the mountain with diamond droplets. The sight of such great beauty brought me a moment of peace amidst the turmoil.

Finally, on June 23, Fred Brooks, the Pro Tem Judge in Superior Court, heard Jennifer's petition. Michael DeLorenzo was held in contempt of court for willfully interfering with the relationship between Jennifer and Maria. Further, the court incorporated the recommendations of the Berk County Family Court, ordering a psychological evaluation of Michael, Jennifer, and Maria DeLorenzo by Dr. Harold Topping. The evaluations were ordered to be completed by September 23. Each party was ordered to pay half of the cost of the evaluation. Michael was restrained from interfering with any visitation Jennifer and Maria scheduled.

At the same time, Craig Walters, Jennifer's attorney, stepped up the pressure for financial disclosure by Michael's current wife, including the income tax returns of both Michael and Gayle DeLorenzo. The statute and court rules regarding petitions for support modification provide that a financial information form must be submitted with the petition for support and that the responding party will execute that form as a part of his or her response. Two main reasons were cited with regard to Gayle and Michael's financial circumstances. Standard 16 of the Oregon State Child Support Schedule states, "There shall be full disclosure of each parent's household financial information." Second Commissioner Amadao had retained jurisdiction from an earlier hearing and indicated discovery should be done, as necessary, to determine Mr. DeLorenzo's financial situation.

Though Gayle resisted the court's request for financial disclosure, a hearing was set for September 6, a motion was made to Compel Discovery, and the court ordered compliance, including the income tax returns filed by Gayle and Michael DeLorenzo from one year earlier.

This elicited an immediate and lengthy response from Michael, which really was, in my opinion, an attempt at stonewalling. On all the statements submitted, the following information was deleted: account numbers, savings account numbers, credit card number, credit limit and balances. Similar information was deleted from a limited number of checks, particularly those in payment of Visa, department stores and oil cards. I pondered what he was hiding.

◆

The relationship between Maria and her mother did not improve after the court ordered Michael to stop interfering. If anything, it deteriorated even more. In addition, neither Maria nor Michael went to their psychological evaluation on September 23.

Jennifer told the court in her declaration on October 31:

"I have not been able to visit with my daughter, nor have I been able to contact her in any meaningful way. After the June 23 order, I attempted to contact my daughter to discuss with her what she would like to do for our visit on July 1. In response to my telephone call, Maria informed me that she could not see me

Saturday, July 1, because family plans had been made at the beginning of that week. I tried to explain to Maria that those plans would have to be changed to a different weekend but her response was something like, 'Oh well, they've already been made and I can't change them.' Later on in the evening, I received a call from Maria. She was agitated and angry at me. She told me that she was very upset about having to be evaluated by a psychiatrist and was under the impression that I was claiming she was 'cuckoo' and forcing her to go. She also told me that she would not go with me on Saturday and that I would just be wasting my gas if I came over to pick her up. Maria also told me that she had talked to her father's attorney and that he had told her she didn't have to go with me if she didn't want to and that no judge is going to make a fourteen-year-old do what she doesn't want to do.

"I tried to explain to Maria that family court routinely recommends an evaluation when a child has been separated from a parent for a long period of time. I told her that I in no way felt she was cuckoo and that her father and I would also have to be evaluated. On the few occasions I have been able to talk to Maria I have expressed my concern for her and her future, that I care for her and love her very much. I know she is under severe pressure from her father not to spend time with me. Despite the court order, I have no contact at all with my daughter. It has been seven months now since I saw her. The last time we were together she was happily making plans for the next time we met.

"With regard to the evaluation to be done by Dr. Topping, I have been informed that the total cost of Dr. Topping's evaluation and report will be approximately $1,500. I will be responsible for one-half of that amount at the time I meet with him. I have already placed $500 with my attorney for this fee and will be able to pay the remaining balance when I meet with Dr. Topping.

"I find it ironic that the respondent claims he cannot afford to pay for Dr. Topping's evaluation, yet in a Family Court Services Parent Questionnaire Evaluation form he completed he states that his monthly gross income is $9,445 and his monthly expenses only

$4,700. The respondent should be found in contempt of the court's June 23 order for not allowing my daughter and I to have a relationship of our own and for not allowing Dr. Topping to conduct the evaluation of Maria and himself which was to be completed by September 23.

"From July 3 to August 12, I tried to reach Maria by telephone many times and got a recorded message indicating that no one was available. On at least ten different occasions I left messages for Maria, but they were not acknowledged or returned. I did, however, speak with Maria once in late July when she called to state she could not be with me the coming Saturday. The fact that she initiated the call, after having been so upset with me in our last conversation, was surprising. Regardless of that, we chatted awhile, until the conversation oddly changed to where I was working. I sensed from Maria an awkwardness in her questions, leading me to wonder about why she was asking. Maria claimed that she had called my office and they stated I no longer worked there. Maria had never telephoned me before at any place other than my home and I feel she was doing what was asked of her by respondent as she was just so awkward and unnatural in how she asked."

◆

On November 16, Craig filed Jennifer's Motion for Contempt *Re: Visitation and Psychiatric Evaluation*.

On November 28, Pro Tem Commissioner Bennis declared, "This is intended to be respondent's last chance to provide the discovery sought by respondent, including Michael and Gayle DeLorenzo's income for the past six months, including pay stubs and social security income verification, tax returns, bank account statements on all Michael and Gayle DeLorenzo's accounts for the last six months, with nothing whited out."

Michael did not comply with the court's directive. Maria did not keep her court ordered visitation on December 9. However, on the evening of December 11, Jennifer received a surprise telephone call from her daughter. "I want to make arrangements to meet," Maria said.

Jennifer's heart skipped a beat. "We have ordered visitation next Saturday. We can talk then, okay?" Jennifer responded hoping the few days would not make a difference.

"Okay, fine. See you then," Maria answered.

Soon afterwards Maria called back. "I can't wait until Saturday. I want to see you tomorrow or the next night. We can meet at Denny's in Westlake," Maria insisted.

Jennifer didn't know what to do. She did not want to be placed in violation of a court order. She also didn't want to lose any time her daughter might want to see her and she didn't want to be placed in a situation where Maria could run in to deliver a message from Mike and then leave with him. Jennifer wanted an opportunity to talk at length with Maria. It had been nearly nine months since they had been alone together. She made an appointment to have dinner with Maria at Denny's, at 6:00 P.M. on December 13.

I urged her to go. Things were deteriorating so badly, what could be worse?

"Sofia, that was one of the worst nights of my life," Jennifer said quietly when we met afterwards. "I had a tiny remnant of hope that Maria and I could come to some kind of understanding and be able to share something together."

"What happened, Jennifer?" I asked. "Tell me about it."

Jennifer's face darkened. "Maria showed up for dinner at Denny's, but so did Michael and Gayle. They were already there when I arrived. I stopped at their table, 'Michael, according to the court directives on visitation, Maria and I are to have that time together alone.' Michael just smiled. At 6'4", he knew I couldn't force him to leave. It was almost more than I could bear. Michael was defying the court directives and I was frightened. I lost my temper, demanding that he leave.

"'We won't,' Michael said. 'We're here to protect Maria.' They sat just two booths away facing Maria. Our long awaited visit turned into a nightmare."

"In what way?" I asked her to tell me the whole story.

"Maria said she wasn't hungry. I was too upset to enjoy my meal but I ordered anyway, just to have something to do. Maria started out by asking me why I hated her dad so much.

"'I don't hate him, so much as I hate the things he's done.' I said trying to explain my feelings.

"'I want to know why. What has he done?' Maria asked."

Jennifer leaned back in the chair and closed her eyes. Her voice had a trance-like quality. "'It began with his mistreatment of me, then my child. He is thoroughly dishonest, and he took you. He also lies and manipulates people. It's not just one thing it's all of it together.' I replied in frustration.

"Maria paused, as though thinking, then replied thoughtfully. 'He's never hit me. I've never even seen him angry.'

"'If that's true, then you're lucky.' I said doubtfully.

"'What do you want, anyway?' Maria asked with a puzzled look on her face.

"'I want us to be together, to have a good relationship. The other thing I want is for you to have a chance for counseling, not because I think you're crazy, as you've been led to believe. I think you need a safe person to talk to, so you can talk your feelings out.'

"'I have a lot of things locked up inside me,' Maria agreed quietly. Then she became agitated. 'No one is ever going to know about them.'"

Jennifer returned to the present. "That was the last time I saw Maria. All I can do now is go to court." Jennifer took a deep breath and changed the subject slightly. "I have so many plans. I thought it through and I've decided to put Maria in a Catholic girl's school until she graduates. I think the structure will be good for her. They seem better equipped to handle problem kids than the public schools do. My sister-in-law says that the key to this is communication, but that's an oversimplification of the matter.

Maria has a completely closed mind now. She's been allowed to do virtually whatever she wanted to for years, as long as she remained loyal to Michael. She needs to learn responsibility, and how to study. According to the school records she's failing in every subject.

"I have figured with what I'll save from the expenses I've had these past few years, I'll be able to afford her counseling, the private schooling, and still be able to get by. Lord knows I've done with less. Maria was complaining about how small the rooms were in my apartment, so I plan to give her the master room and I'll move into the little guest bedroom."

As Jennifer chatted on and on, I wondered to myself how she could have such unrealistic dreams. Couldn't she see how completely troubled Maria was? She showed no apparent love or sympathy for Jennifer. Her every thought was concerned with her father and his need for her. It was a testimonial to Father McNeilly's concern that he was willing to pull strings to get Maria accepted at the Holy Communion School, but it would take a miracle to get her to stay there.

I felt I had to inject some reality into Jennifer's rose-colored dreams. "Jennifer, I want you to listen to yourself. Maria is going to need a lot of therapy and counseling, and so are you. You need to learn how to deal with some serious problems Maria is going to bring with her. You can't go on putting yourself last in everything and expect to nurture her respect for you as a parent. You need a decent chance at happiness, too. Giving her your bedroom isn't the answer. She is not a princess, and she won't be a guest in your home. She needs to face economic reality and learn to associate rewards and success with her own hard work. Your other child is becoming strong and resourceful because she learned those things. I'm not trying to be unkind, but it scares me to see you talking like it's going to be peaches and cream. It just won't happen."

Jennifer didn't say anything for a long time. When she spoke I realized I had shattered a fantasy she created to help her get through this tough time. "I know that," Jennifer said softly. "It's just that I'm so scared for Maria. The evaluation by Dr. Topping doesn't appear any closer to occurring than when we first requested it. Michael has manipulated her mind and emotions, so much—I don't believe anymore in the things I had hoped for. I know you're right and that the only thing that is worth fighting for now is to get her into therapy so she doesn't end up like Michael. I can't imagine how she will treat the men that will come into her life when she's an adult. All she's ever seen is that you use people to your own advantage, take what you want and leave without remorse or conscience. Still I can't help hoping and praying she'll come home with me. And, there are other things I'm having to deal with."

I sat there for a few moments absorbing the things Jennifer shared. The pain and loneliness of her suffering as a mother were beyond words of sympathy.

Finally I spoke. "Jennifer," I said, "what will you be asking for when you go to trial?"

She sighed heavily. "Custody of Maria and having the back child support dismissed. In lieu of all that, enforced visitation. I know fulfilling my first desire will be like pulling a rabbit out of a hat," Jennifer said despondently.

"But you still want it," I went on.

She nodded. "I know it's possible, what I don't know is what to expect with Maria."

"It could be difficult, perhaps hellish if you get it."

"Yes, when Mike reads the psychiatrist's evaluation of himself and Maria, he is going to prime Maria saying, 'See what they've done? They've lied about us. If they make you go with her, you just run away. They can't make you stay.' I expect him to bring her to court, he's done that before. I don't want her to go through it," Jennifer cried.

"I have the opposite feeling," I said slowly, my own emotions welling up. "I think she should be in court for every minute of testimony, to hear lie after lie of his refuted with the truth. She's never heard the truth."

A memory suddenly flashed through my mind of my childhood friend Dulcie. Once again I saw the chicken coop in which she and her parents had lived. I remembered the outrage I had felt. Again, the same angry feeling struck me. For just as surely as that family had been victimized by society, these women had been victimized by Michael. Both had been sacrificed to oppressors who were stronger and more powerful than they were.

I couldn't get the anguish of Jennifer's words out of my mind the rest of that night. I had to find a way to help her and the rest of the women Michael had harmed. During the next few days I searched out more information on Michael from court records and newspapers. I gathered them together in a brief case. I decided to give Detective Jensen the legal papers carefully organized by date and made notes for myself regarding the contents.

This time I was determined to do something about what I knew. In the next few weeks I spent every non-working hour at the courthouse seeking and reading voluminous files about Michael DeLorenzo and searching out bits of information by talking to his associates and friends. Each piece of information I found seemed to build upon the last. A bank's investigation of corporate fraud led to income tax evasion charges. The FBI's investigation, and Jennifer's pregnancy, led to a bitter dissolution of Michael and Anna's twenty-odd year marriage. This ushered in Michael's suicide attempt, his stalking, death threats to Anna and any of their children who tried to protect her. I realized it didn't end there. No one knew that better than I did. Michael's life of intimidation was just beginning.

I was reading the account of the forgery and credit card fraud case brought by Alex Solimine, when my attention suddenly focused on a small but immensely important detail which shed light on why Michael was so eager to reclaim the wedding rings he had given me. I quickly went back to reread the case from the beginning. Michael DeLorenzo had been prosecuted for two counts of theft and two counts of forgery by the Berk County Prosecuting Attorney's office, DPA Carl Gordon.

Case No. 45-1-03676-4

SUPPLEMENTAL CERTIFICATION FOR DETER-
MINATION OF PROBABLE CAUSE
Count II

That Barbara R. Kern is a Deputy Prosecuting Attorney for Berk County and is familiar with the police report and investigation conducted in Portland Police Department case No. 45D03322 and 45B7439;

That this case contains the following upon which this motion for the determination of probable cause is made;

About the end of June, Samuel Hagman, owner of Sam's Jewelry, located in Portland, Berk County, Oregon received an order from his long time friend Michael DeLorenzo for two wedding rings and an engagement set worth $2,700.00 on July 1, DeLorenzo picked up the rings and paid Hagman with check No. 556 for $2,700 written on the Second Pacific Bank account number 0325700 for ICF National Limited. When Hagman questioned DeLorenzo about the solvency of the ICF account, DeLorenzo assured Hagman that his import business was doing well.

A few days later the check was returned unpaid, and the bank informed Hagman that they could not locate the ICF account. The bank then found that DeLorenzo had opened the account on February 2, with a $300 deposit, and that the bank had closed the account on May 23, for an overdraft of $208.74.

Hagman tried to locate DeLorenzo to obtain payment for the rings, but was unable to do so. DeLorenzo never made any effort to pay for the rings or to return them.

The other counts involved forgeries of Alex Solimine's name on credit card purchases Michael made on a credit card he had stolen from his long time friend and benefactor, Alex Solimine. The sentencing Judge Frank A. Locano sentenced DeLorenzo on count I (theft 1 degree) to nine months of total confinement in the Berk County jail. The court also sentenced him to six months of total confinement for each count II, (theft) count III, (forgery) and count IV, (forgery to run concurrently). The court ordered the defendant to pay restitution of $3,528.30, be allowed work release, if eligible, to pay court costs and victim penalty assessment and abide by all standard conditions.

I saw it wasn't long before Michael was back in court, in front of Judge Locano again. This was case No. 33-4-03651-2.

Reading the next lines and picturing the scene in my mind, I could not stop laughing. This time he was answering the court in response to having forged a letter from a physician in an attempt to gain leniency in a Superior Court sentencing in front of Judge Frank Locano in May of that same year. He was arraigned and the Omnibus Hearing was set for August 10. Before this could happen however, the following article appeared in the Portland Journal.

MAN ALIVE! TROUBLES DO PILE UP

A Portland man who allegedly tried to gain leniency from a judge by saying he was a "dying man" has been charged with forging a doctor's letter that said he was gravely ill with cancer.

When Michael DeLorenzo appeared before Berk County Superior Court Judge Frank Locano May 13 for sentencing on guilty pleas to charges of theft and forgery, according to authorities, he presented a letter on a doctor's stationery.

Prosecutors said the letter indicated that DeLorenzo faced radical surgery.

"Your honor, I am a dying man," DeLorenzo said in open court, according to prosecutors.

DeLorenzo's attorney asked for an exceptional sentence because of his client's physical condition.

Judge Locano, concerned over incarcerating a man with health problems, asked that DeLorenzo call the physician, on the court's phone and set up an appointment.

DeLorenzo appeared to dial the phone then said the doctor wouldn't be in for several days; according to prosecutors, Judge Locano then continued the sentencing hearing until May 24.

But Deputy Prosecutor Carl Gordon became suspicious and called the doctor, who said the letter was totally fabricated, according to court papers.

The physician said he had seen DeLorenzo only once for an unrelated condition.

Prosecutors said that on May 24, DeLorenzo apologized to the court and was sentenced to nine months in jail on the prior charges.

As I replaced the paperwork in the appropriate files, a thought came to me that there was something else, something I had read in this huge stack of legal papers that dealt with Michael's work release connected to this case. Now all I had to do was find it. I went back over the legal drafts and came across Berk County Police Department case No. 37-8466, which concerned the business partnership between Michael and Alex Solimine.

Solimine had allowed DeLorenzo to use his credit card several times to take clients to lunch. In September, Solimine discovered several unauthorized charges had been made on his card by DeLorenzo and had that card canceled. He also told DeLorenzo that he no longer had permission to use his credit card. MasterCard sent Solimine a new credit card, number 4379-0143-1177-2136, during that same September, but Solimine never received it in the mail.

On October 2, October 3, October 4, October 6, and October 17, Michael DeLorenzo went to Family Counselors located in Portland Oregon and told his childhood friend Ogdon Leeds, that he had permission to use Solimine's credit card. On those occasions, Dr. Leeds gave DeLorenzo a total of $730 in cash advances on Solimine's credit card account. Of course, Solimine had not given DeLorenzo permission to use the card or to obtain money from his account.

DeLorenzo's whereabouts are unknown at this time. A warrant at $3,000 bail should be issued.

An informational report filled out by Liza Bailey, Berk County Police Department stated; Less than a week later, it was reported to the police that DeLorenzo took a personal credit card belonging to his business associate, Alex Solimine. Solimine said his credit card was stolen out of his desk drawer and used all over Berk County without his permission. DeLorenzo had also used the card in Portland at Family Counselors. Dr. Leeds identified DeLorenzo as the person who used Solimine's credit card at his place of business. DeLorenzo is nowhere to be found and is still in possession of the credit card.

I read and reread the dates all this had happened realizing Michael had been living at my house at that time. How could Ogdon Leeds say he didn't know where Michael was when he had called us at my home many times? I knew he still had both my telephone number and address, and Michael dropped by his office constantly.

As I looked carefully over the papers again, I also realized much of the intimidation and innuendo Michael had used against Jennifer, both verbally and in declarations centered around Dr. Ogdon Leeds, was fabricated. He was always presented to the court as a professional, unimpeachable, witness against Jennifer. The fact that there were no other corroborating witnesses to any of the allegations was glaringly apparent when a single person read all of the documentation and rebuttal. Unfortunately, the information presented to the court regarding the custody was seldom heard by the same judge twice. This worked in Michael's favor. Inconsistencies and outright lies were often overlooked. When Jennifer railed at the unfairness or ugliness of the materials being presented to the court by opposing counsel as "truth," her attorney advised her that when it came time to go to court, the real truth would come out and that she should not to be concerned about it. Jennifer, however, had good reason to be concerned because it went beyond the court case. According to several accounts, Michael was showing his slanderous testimonials to their daughter, Maria, with devastating effects.

I could not imagine why anyone would show those kinds of things to a child, especially with all of the falsehoods and degrading statements regarding her mother.

As I read on, I saw that between that declaration in March, and November of the same year, Maria's responsiveness to Jennifer and her attitude in general had dramatically changed. Michael maintained absolute and complete control of Maria. It was obvious to me that no visitation had been allowed, no phone calls were made without him being at Maria's side to monitor what was said. There was no empathy for what Maria might have felt or wanted. She was expected to remain loyal. Jennifer was the enemy.

When I got home, carrying with me the documents I had copied, I picked up the telephone and dialed Jennifer's number. She wasn't home. I left a message for her to call me and went back to reading more documents.

When I was finished reading, I did chores for a few hours. Sometime later that day I came across several newspaper clippings in one of the boxes of papers I had accumulated. Most of them dealt with the criminal activities of Michael DeLorenzo. However, two of the newspaper articles from the Portland Journal, given to me by my friend Bart, told of a lawsuit by a woman who was awarded $95,999 damages by a Superior Court jury against Ogdon Leeds.

According to the articles, Mrs. Carol Rogers sued Leeds and the Ryone hospital district that has jurisdiction over the town of Coldridge, contending her emotional and mental health was severely damaged in two years of counseling . . . Mrs. Rogers testified Dr. Leeds had intercourse with her and gave her $80 for an abortion after she became pregnant . . . Alan, her husband, was told by his wife that Leeds impregnated her, and he confronted the therapist, threatening a lawsuit of his own and asking for the return of $4,805 in counseling fees. Leeds asked for ten days, then made payment at a shopping center.

Counsel for the hospital argued that Leeds was not acting within the scope of his employment.

Mrs. Rogers contended the hospital was negligent in hiring him and should not have done so in light of his previous termination as chief social worker at the Keats Mental Health Center for Buck and Richards Counties, and as director of medical social work at Clinton's Orthopedic Hospital. Back at the library and then at both institutions I discovered upon further research that these were positions where the titles were larger than the jobs. Leeds wrote his own job description and job title making it appear that he was a full-time employee. Actually Leeds worked part-time.

When Jennifer returned my call, I had, in my mind, a great many questions but only one for her. "Jennifer I'm making some progress but I need to know something. When Judge Locano sentenced Michael for his forgery conviction, he asked for work release. Where did Michael serve his work release time?"

"At the Family Counseling Center in Portland. He was released to Ogdon Leeds," Jennifer replied.

"That's just what I surmised. Forgive me for not explaining all this to you now. I'll be back in touch soon. I have to do some legwork. Just keep a good thought."

Before Jennifer could ask more questions, questions for which I had no answers, I said goodbye.

I needed to reopen my search and find stronger proof of Michael DeLorenzo's duplicity.

That search centered on Michael DeLorenzo's life history. He had told so many different stories. There were things about his past I had to know. I interviewed more people and looked up more records and documents on his education, naval service, and marriages. Many of the scraps of information I gathered on Michael contradicted one another. Sorting out what was true from what was false was difficult. Still, I was able to confirm some facts.

Michael DeLorenzo was born in Haverford, Texas. Much of his background is unclear because so many versions have been presented in court documents and interviews. However, it appears that Michael was the last of three children and the only son of an Irish mother and an Italian father. The father was a hard worker, but not too well appreciated by the mother because of his periodic drinking episodes. He died when Michael was eight-years-old. After his father's death, Michael was expected to help his mother out economically. He earned money carrying newspapers, working on small farms, and cutting lawns during the summer. He gave his earnings to his mother and she would periodically give him some change for his needs and to go to the movies. Although the home was kept exceptionally neat and clean Michael felt ashamed of his circumstances. According to some accounts and some letters from his mother, Michael was, "something of a problem all his years. Though he was extremely bright, Michael never seemed to learn from his mistakes and blamed others for problems which he himself created." As his mother put it, "He always spent his time dreaming and scheming." She said, "It was just one scam after another, none of his plans had a basis in reality." She claimed, "Michael has been impervious to the everyday lessons of life."

Like much of his history, Michael's military history also varied according to which account one read. The United States Naval records reveal that he was in the service only fifteen months and served as a cook during that time. He was given a hardship discharge after repeated petitions from Michael and his mother.

Michael's psychological profile, on record, describes him as "high strung, tense, and apprehensive though he gives an outward impression of composure. Generally, the more tense he is, the more verbose he becomes. When the clarity of a situation becomes obscured, Michael becomes so anxious that his own thinking becomes obscured and he finds it difficult to relate to detail and becomes repetitive in his thinking."

The profile goes on to report, "During his first marriage to Anna Corda he suffered spells of impotency and chronic depression. He is what would be considered a punitive self-disciplining ego. He has suffered insomnia since childhood."

Throughout his marriage, Michael worked only periodically with long stretches of unemployment during which the family was supported by his wife Anna with help from the growing children and Michael's mother. He suffered periods of deep depression and violent outbreaks of temper. Michael didn't devote a lot of time to his children—hours necessary to build intimacy and trust. They knew him as an authority figure more feared than loved. Anna, who was Catholic, and many of her contemporaries grew up naive about men in general and were taught at home and in church that the father was the absolute voice of authority.

Further, one report said that Michael has a distorted view of himself as honorable, hardworking, and set upon. Unable to recognize how he orchestrates his own disasters, he came to see Anna, the one who supported him, as the enemy. He had financial problems throughout his adult life and dealt with money, whether it was his or others in an adolescent way. He was quick to explain that his difficulties were the result of what other people had done to him. His enemies list included his mother, business partners who cheated him, and a boss who fired him for no reason.

When Anna was young and still believed in Michael, he was her whole life. All she ever wanted was to have a good Catholic family life and be a good wife. He was so bright. He had so much potential. She thought if she would just be supportive enough, eventually he would succeed. Michael could be bigger than life. When he treated you well the sky was the limit. She didn't recognize his behavior as an illness, but she soon found out it was either feast or famine. There was little middle ground. Life was either full speed ahead or you were tiptoeing around because he was unemployed again and in a deep depression.

Failure was a deep injury to Michael. Anna grew up in a generation when men were preoccupied with their careers and their financial success. Added to that was the crushing life he had lived with his mother after his father died from a lingering illness resulting from a mining accident. Michael took his loss very hard.

Because of these losses, his marriage became so troubled that family counseling was sought and then mental health counseling as well. As Michael became more belligerent, Anna became a victim in her own home, growing more and more fearful and insecure, finally questioning her own sanity and desire to hold on to life. Michael criticized her day and night when they were alone and in front of relatives and friends alike, as being unstable and stupid.

A detailed picture of the real Michael began to emerge. I thought about Alan Harrington's book, *Psychopaths*. How well, in my opinion, Michael fit Harrington's description.

"The psychopath doesn't suffer as much as he makes others suffer. Since he is freed of inhibitions, his impulses are said immediately to spill over into action. He takes what he wants when he wants it . . . He may lie glibly and show little, if any embarrassment when he is caught out."

Michael's history seemed, to me, a classic profile. Still I had to prove this truth and my search was stymied.

Then, a few nights later, Jennifer came over unexpectedly. "Tuesday I got out some boxes that had been in storage for some time," she said, her words rushing together, "and I ran across some old tapes. The eight-tracks were so old I discarded them but then," she paused and sighed, "I ran across a tape I'd never seen before."

"Was there any marking on it?" I asked.

"The only notation," Jennifer said, "was the handwritten initials MDL."

"Did you play it?" I asked.

"Of course," she laughed. "Wouldn't you?"

"Of course," I repeated.

She sighed. "It was Michael bullying and badgering and manipulating his distraught first wife, Anna."

"Why would he leave you that tape? In fact, why would he have taped that?" I asked, surprised. "It's like a cat playing with an injured mouse. He is so insensitive and sick. What possible use could that tape have served?"

Jennifer shook her head. She handed me the tape. "Here, don't worry about returning it. This is a copy. I gave my attorney the original."

I slipped the cassette into my purse, and knowing the contents would be upsetting, I made a mental note to listen to them that weekend on my way to camp out on Mt. Saint Helens.

That Friday, before dawn, I threw my gear into the Blazer, added extra clothes for warmth, and double checked to make certain my camera and hiking shoes hadn't been forgotten. On the seat beside me I placed a briefcase of documents and the cassette tape Jennifer had given me. Driving is a perfect time to arrange one's thoughts and I had many long hours of uninterrupted driving ahead.

I plugged in the tape and pressed the play button. I shuddered as Michael's menacing voice filled the car as he talked about his life with his first wife.

I listened in stunned silence as the cassette divulged the true ugliness of their life together. I heard the tragic voices of Lucia, Michael, and Anna's daughter. Lucia was trying to act as an intermediary so that the repressed violence of her father would not explode. Anna was overwhelmed in both mind and spirit by long, stressful years with Michael, and making desperate pleas to finally be left alone. Michael's controlled rage was apparent as he relentlessly baited his wife and daughter, claiming he wanted to repair the marriage and loved them both.

I shuddered as I felt Anna's pervading sadness as she softly responded. Her lack of hope and acceptance touched me so deeply that I could not stop the tears which rose to my eyes.

Then, as I thought of the lasting effects of Michael's words on his obviously gentle and empathetic young daughter—who not only was caught in the middle of her parent's painful discussion, but had to be feeling her own pain—I too, like Anna, felt overwhelmed.

Painful images passed though my mind. For these women, like me, like all the others Michael had hurt so deeply, had loved him. We had all tried to help him, only to be rewarded by his cruelty. The words he was saying to Anna and Lucia could as easily have been said to Jennifer, Alicia, Gayle or I. To all of us he had claimed his financial problems were caused by every one except himself. To all of us he had pleaded for money. And we all had given. We gave until our security for the future was gone, until our homes were threatened, our children stolen from, and our very selves became depleted and depressed.

As he accused Anna over and over of treating him like dirt, I felt that he was really saying she *was* dirt—and that he would accuse and label us all the same derogatory way. How many times had he snarled degrading curses at one or the other of us? How many times had he labeled us crazy or twisted our words. Weren't we all, when married to him and then having found out the truth, miserable and depressed?

I felt as if I could stand no more, and yet I could not stop listening. Anna's story was perhaps the worst. For she had endured the pain more years than the rest of us. However, as I heard her beaten down and terrorized, the stories of each of the women Michael had tortured whirled about in my thoughts. The ugly words only increased their similarities.

It was almost a shock when the tape suddenly clicked off. I felt disgusted. The pleasure this man took in destroying others was only offset by the justification he gave himself. Anna was right. The only feelings that mattered to him were Michael DeLorenzo's own.

No wonder he was afraid to present himself to Dr. Topping the psychiatrist. With his training there was too great a chance Michael would be unmasked. Michael had unsuccessfully tried to have the court remove or replace Dr. Topping as the evaluating doctor.

I tried to enjoy the rest of the weekend, but no matter how beautiful the scenery, how warm the blazing fire, I shuddered as I kept replaying, in my mind, the recording of those bitter cold words and thought of the shattered lives they represented.

Not long afterward, I learned that Michael attempted to persuade Dr. Topping to evaluate Maria over the telephone, rather than in the privacy of the office. He wanted to control her responses. Dr. Topping refused. The court gave Michael two weeks to present Maria for evaluation or be held in contempt of court. He scheduled Maria to see Dr. Topping two weeks later.

The next time I heard from Jennifer, I learned Maria had threatened to run away if the girl had to continue visitation with her mother. Letters protesting forced visitation had been presented to the court on her behalf. Jennifer was completely discouraged. I listened as Jennifer confided her fear that the judge who ultimately would hear her case would briefly skim or not read the case file at all. "And even if he does, how could a person be able to discern the truth when so many lies have been presented in sworn documents?" she asked wearily.

Chapter Eighteen

Gayle's Story

*A*s I delved deeper and deeper into Michael's disheveled past, I realized it was not only Jennifer and I who had been hurt. All the other women Michael had used and deceived until they didn't know the difference between truth and fantasy, were also injured.

Two years before meeting Michael, Gayle Higgins, a striking redhead with one teenage son, Jesse, had just gotten her life back on the right track after facing the emotional and financial problems of divorce and the death of a daughter killed by a drunk driver.

She had a job she liked as a receptionist at the Livewell Nursing Home and had a nest egg which, if she never remarried, she planned to keep for her retirement. Her home mortgage was just about paid off. In addition, she had an IRA, investments at Ronaldson Alter Inc., a liquid bank account, and her father had just passed away—leaving half his estate "to take care of mama" and the rest to his two children.

Because her early life had been hard and there was little money, Gayle had always been a saver. Her habit had turned out to be a good one. She wasn't rich, but finally she was financially secure. However, the week of her fortieth birthday reminded Gayle just how lonely she really was. There were plenty of dates but there was no one in her life who really mattered.

And then, she met Michael DeLorenzo.

It was a warm, balmy June day and Gayle had gone to work at Livewell wishing she was going on vacation to some wonderful island with someone she loved.

Sitting at her desk behind a three-quarter wall which had a small opening so that the residents or their families could visit. Gayle was typing reports. She didn't see the handsome, dark-haired man walk over until he tapped her on the shoulder and started talking. "I'm Michael DeLorenzo," he said. "Hello."

She looked up into deep blue eyes and felt like she had walked outside to admire the day and been engulfed by the sky.

"Hello yourself," she said.

As he ran his hand through thick wavy hair she noticed he wore a gold wedding band and frowned. Following her glance he shook his head, "Actually I'm divorced and have custody of my twelve year old daughter Maria. The reason I'm wearing a wedding band is that I'm," he flushed and went on, "well, I'm going to Hawaii, a lot of the women there want to buy me drinks and I'm just not into that stuff."

Gayle could not stop herself from laughing, "Now you know what us females have to contend with."

He threw his head back and laughed with her, "I can appreciate that."

Then explaining that he had come to see his mother, he excused himself. "I wish I could stay but mom looks forward to these visits, I don't want to disappoint her." On his way out he stopped back to see her. "I wish I wasn't going away but I'll be back soon."

When Gayle went home that evening she immediately called her sister. "Lee, I've met a man," Gayle said, "and if God is willing he will be my husband."

Two weeks later Michael DeLorenzo came back to see his mother, stopped by Gayle's desk and asked for her telephone number. A few days afterward he called to invite her out for a coffee which led to dinner and a long intimate talk. That is—he talked while Gayle sat entranced, listening as Michael described his past life.

About his naval service he told her, "I was in a submarine off Alaska, on top with the officers. It was torpedoed and," he paused for a moment his eyes moist, "the Japanese killed three of the officers and though I was wounded, I got to the control room, submerged the sub and handled it. I was due for the medal of—what was it?—the silver star for bravery." He looked away, "But I never accepted it."

"Why not?" she asked.

"Because," he looked back into her eyes, "because I felt I killed people," he shuddered. "I couldn't forget that."

A half an hour or so passed. He kept talking. He looked sad talking about his wonderfully long marriage, the one he'd shattered by his "one night stand with Jennifer Surel," who he termed, "that awful woman who never did anything right except to make our beautiful daughter, Maria." He talked about his marriage to Alicia and the millions of dollars which she was trying to get from him with the aid of a barracuda attorney. Lastly, he spoke of his airplane and boats and very successful business ventures.

When he finished Gayle told him about her own past including her daughter who had died. Maybe she told him too much, but she couldn't seem to stop herself from confiding in this wonderfully sensitive man.

As they left the restaurant, Gayle impulsively took his hand as he walked her to her car. Gallantly, Michael opened the door, she got in, and he closed it. When Gayle rolled down the window to say goodbye he leaned over, brought his face close to hers and kissed her passionately.

After that they met often and spent long evenings dining, dancing, or lying on the thick blue carpet in her living room, listening to music. "I'm a rug rat," he explained which seemed a wonderful coincidence because so was she.

Eventually Michael introduced her to his daughter, Maria, who looked sad and waifish and for whom Gayle felt an immediate liking. She introduced him to her son Jesse. At Christmas, Maria moved to Gayle's house. Michael had not yet moved in, because Maria was so young and Gayle wanted her relationship with the girl to be kind of special. But soon a lonely Michael moved in with them.

He borrowed Gayle's credit card to buy presents for Maria. Somehow he forgot to give it back. A short while later Gayle and he began making plans for their wedding.

There was talk of going to Bermuda and places he and Maria had stayed, but these plans evaporated. Gayle and Michael were married in Utah. Although Gayle wasn't aware of it at the time, he charged the trip to her credit card. When she did find out, Michael explained that Alicia had tied up his money and he would pay Gayle back very soon.

Of course, she believed him.

Sometime afterward he told Gayle a little about his other problems, however, he didn't mention they were criminal or with the IRS.

For a while they were blissfully happy. Gayle grew close to Maria and Michael to her son. The four of them became a family. It was during this period that Jennifer Surel came back into Maria's life and filed suit.

Loyal to her husband and always trusting what he said about Jennifer, Gayle had even agreed to let him borrow from her son's trust account to fight the suit, to fight Jennifer who Gayle believed was the enemy.

"Don't worry I'll pay you back very soon," he promised.

Gayle, believing in Michael, had given a statement on Michael's and Maria's behalf against that terrible woman. Maria's natural mother was unfit and had a violent temper.

Many of these things were coached by Michael in front of Maria, and afterward Gayle regretted her statement. In her statement, Gayle said, "Neither I nor Michael have in any way tried to influence Maria or to discourage her from seeing Jennifer Surel."

Around the same time Michael asked her if she minded his testifying in court regarding Alex Solimine against his mistress.

"Of course I wouldn't mind," Gayle said sympathetically.

"You really are the most understanding person," Michael said softly and took her in his arms.

No more was mentioned of that case.

It was only when Michael was sentenced to jail that he was forced to tell Gayle of his own problems and even then it was a half truth. "It's only for three months dear," he told her. "It's because Galveston didn't file the papers in time. Otherwise, I would have been exonerated."

"Michael, what is this all about?" Gayle asked.

"I'm not a criminal," he insisted. "Darling you know I wanted to leave and terminated my position with Alex as of May. Well, I wrote a few checks to pay some debts and I guess the account was already closed. Because Alex was angry with me for giving him notice, he filed charges."

Once again Gayle was supportive, even writing a letter on Michael's behalf to the judge begging him to release her husband.

Reading the Portland papers a short while later, Gayle learned about Michael's own letter. It was ostensibly from his doctor begging for clemency, and said Michael was terminally ill. This was the letter that was later found to be a forgery and for which Michael served more time in jail.

By the time Michael was released, Maria was beginning to confide in Gayle. Maria said she had never been in Bermuda. When Gayle mentioned this to Michael in front of his daughter Michael said, staring directly at the girl, "You just don't remember or maybe, Maria, you want to suppress it."

After that, the situation deteriorated. The reasons were many and varied. Among them, Michael took money from his mother's private account at the nursing home and had extra checks printed for the bank account he shared with Gayle, so she wouldn't be able to track the depletion of funds by check number sequence.

Michael had the statements of the credit cards, obtained by forging Gayle's name, sent to his private post office box.

Gayle was embarrassed by Michael's criminal behavior and her gullibility. She had truly believed the stories and justifications he gave her for not being liquid. Only after the last of her money was gone and she was forced to face the reality of her plight did she begin to investigate the things Michael told her.

Finally, Gayle took a trip to Florida to think things over. When she returned, Michael told her he was flown by Mr. Dodenberg by helicopter to review a resort—a supposed construction job. Gayle talked to Mr. Dodenberg, and he didn't fly him. In fact, he hasn't spoken with Michael for quite a while.

Then there was another job. The Porter job, back in Chicago. The employer's name was Mr. Olin. Michael said he really wanted to pursue this job. She even had a letter written to her saying that he wanted to pursue the Porter job.

According to Michael, he had met with Mr. Olin and Catherine Richards in Portland. Gayle called Mr. Olin herself. When Gayle got him on the phone, Olin thought she was crazy. She said, "Mr. Olin, I understand your position, but I'm calling because I want to know the truth." That's when Olin made a statement that he never was in Portland and he never met Catherine Richards. He had spoken with Mr. DeLorenzo on the telephone because Mr. DeLorenzo requested some information and that's all. When Gayle confronted Michael about him telephoning Mr. Olin, he said, "No, we met flesh to flesh."

When Michael flatly denied everything Gayle had been told, her eyes began opening. She searched further. That is when she discovered the bigamy. At the courthouse she found out not just about Alicia, but me as well. And that was when Gayle found out the reason why the annulment of Michael's marriage to me was taking so long. It was because I did not want to pay for the annulment.

Months went by and gradually there were more and more disclosures from Maria and the law. Gayle grew further disillusioned, and by the following Christmas season, Gayle had had enough.

This time Michael realized Gayle was finished. He packed a few bags and left the house with Maria, who put a note under the tree for Gayle:

> Mother, Merry Christmas. Sorry I couldn't get you a real card (no money). You've been a really loving, caring, understanding person and mother. You're one in a million. I'll miss you very much. I'll always remember you, no matter what. Sorry for all of the heartache and problems me and my father have put you through! And like I said before he never pays, if he never pays you back, when, and if I have enough money, I'll pay you back. Keep in touch, see ya.
>
> —Maria
> P.S. I felt selfish taking the present under the tree, that's why it's still there.

Michael obviously had no such qualms about his selfishness, he took his gift with him, and among other things: a microwave oven he had bought Gayle, stereo equipment, and even Gayle's family Bible.

Not long after Michael moved, Jesse, Gayle's son spotted him in their neighborhood. Jesse, who had just learned to drive, followed Michael in Gayle's car. Michael drove everywhere trying to elude him but couldn't. Jesse was very angry over the money Michael had taken and the debts he had left for Jesse's mother to pay. Despite the turns and twists, he stayed on Michael's car's tail. Finally Michael went to the Eastgate Park and Ride. He drove to the far corner where it was unlighted and parked with his headlights off. Jesse pulled into the lot near the entrance. Afraid to come closer, Jesse sat watching Michael. As he got out of his car, Michael took something metal from the trunk and stood with his legs apart in a menacing manner.

Smart enough to be very scared by this time, Jesse turned the key in the ignition, stepped on the gas, and drove quickly away.

Jennifer was almost elated the next time we spoke. Dr. Topping's evaluation came back refuting Michael's accusations. His final conclusion about her was, "In total, Jennifer does not appear to have emotional problems of a magnitude that would adversely impact her ability to have ongoing visitation with her daughter."

I decided a celebration might be good for both Jennifer and me. I opted for dinner at a Greek restaurant not far from her apartment. I picked Jennifer up an hour later.

"Try the village salad if you're unsure of the menu," I suggested. "It's the one I fixed for you last summer."

"I trust you. Order for me."

"At least tell me what you don't like," I protested. Jennifer laughed and went back to her menu. After much discussion we each chose a village salad, moussaka, and rice pilaf.

When our Chianti arrived I raised my glass. "Here's to better days ahead," I said and touched Jennifer's wine glass with mine. Gayle's announcement that she and Michael had separated gave us an additional boost of energy and hope, though both of us were tired of the endless wait for trial. Nearly four years had passed since the first court appearance.

"I can't help but wonder if Gayle's last experiences with Michael will effect her testimony—whether she'll support you now."

"Every time I say I've given up trying to figure people out I find myself trying to do just that. I don't know what to expect from any quarter anymore," Jennifer said.

"You know, Jennifer, I live with a thousand questions. For every one answer, ten more appear." I shook my head. "Most of all I wonder why Gayle doesn't press charges against Michael for credit card fraud and put him in jail where he belongs."

"It's like the questions I've asked myself in the past. Why did I keep on believing Michael long after I learned what he was? Part of me didn't want to give up the dream. It's too devastating to face the truth," Jennifer replied.

"Have you ever read a book called, *Men Who Hate Women, and the Women Who Love Them*?" I asked. "It was written by a woman psychiatrist who did a lot of counseling for abused women. It's fascinating. But even after reading it, I couldn't completely understand the people she described. I could pity them for their problems, but I don't really understand. Why should a woman be so self-destructive that she'll assist the very person who wants to destroy her?" I asked, perplexed.

Jennifer shook her head. "I'm probably the last person who could answer that question for you," Jennifer sighed. "It sounds like a book I should read."

Just then, the freckled young waitress arrived with a tempting dessert tray, precariously balanced. The Baklava looked enticing and cheese cake topped with strawberries looked delicious. With our customary lack of restraint we decided to share both.

"I'm so glad my evaluation with Dr. Topping went well," Jennifer said after we had finished.

"Good! I know Maria had her evaluation. Have you gotten her results yet?"

"No. We won't get anything until Michael goes in and he's using every delay tactic he can muster by asking that the court not force the evaluation. He's trying to get the court to accept someone he's personally selected rather than Dr. Topping."

"Which means a doctor who doesn't know him or one who has already been snowed," I interjected.

"I don't think the court's going to be influenced. He's pushed it about as far as he can. He's in contempt already."

"Were you worried about your evaluation?" I asked.

"I was a nervous wreck," Jennifer replied. "So much depended upon it. I just went in with the attitude of being completely honest and hoped for the best. It helped that I trust Dr. Topping's reputation. Craig would only recommend the best and he was pleased with the court's decision. But the big question remains—how long will it take to get Michael into Topping's office?"

"We'll have to sweat that out but..." I smiled at her encouragingly. "Things are looking up. Just hang in there. Look at the changes in just the past few months. We've been complaining about the endless postponements, but if the trial had been held before Gayle and Michael split, her testimony would've been much different. Things are only getting better."

◆

It was a full six months and many court motions later, when Dr. Topping finally was able to evaluate Michael DeLorenzo, and at Jennifer's request, did a reevaluation of Maria. His report on Michael was insightful:

HAROLD TOPPING, M.D., Ph.D.
111 Clacksmas Street, Suite 412
Portland, Oregon 87218

July 18, 1990

Byron Hadon Esq.   Craig Walters Esq.
Attorney at Law   Attorney at Law
310 Century Avenue   1101 Title Bldg.

Portland, OR 87208   640 1st Avenue
                                      Portland, OR 87208

RE: MICHAEL DeLORENZO

Dear Messrs. Hadon and Walters:

This report is based on a psychiatric evaluation of Michael De-
Lorenzo conducted at my office. Very extensive background
material accumulated over the past few months, submitted by
both attorneys and both clients were reviewed prior to this
session. The specific foci of this session were to provide an
overall assessment of Michael's emotional state, to attempt to
understand his role in the dynamics that have led to difficulty
in visitation between Jennifer and Maria DeLorenzo, to evaluate Michael's parenting abilities and to make any recommendations pertinent to visitation between mother and
daughter.

In addition to the clinical evaluation, Michael took the
MMPI-2. The clinical report and profile generated from this
testing will be included in this evaluation package. Any additional comments thought necessary after review of the
MMPI-2 report will be added at the end of this report.

Michael is presented as a tall (6'4"), well proportioned (201
pounds), man who appeared a few years younger than his
stated chronologic age. He clearly is a very vital and active person. I believe that Michael was fairly defensive and moderated
his responses to questions that were asked. He appears to take
very little responsibility for his problematic actions and tends
to blame others or situations for problems that he has had. My
contacts with Michael, including affidavits and letters that he
has written indicate to me that he uses many passive-aggressive
tactics to deal with life and also has little if any compunction
against lying. Michael appears to be an extremely manipulative
person who will do virtually anything legal or illegal to accom-
plish his ends. He has a very faulty conscience, one that clearly
is a very bad example for a child to be exposed to, one that has

landed him in trouble repeatedly in his life. Michael appears to be an extremely intelligent man whose personality problems have prevented him from consistently utilizing that intelligence in socially appropriate ways. While we might be able to excuse any one of the many poor decisions or faulty uses of judgment that Michael has exercised, the net sum total of all of these problems is considerable.

His insight and judgment appear to be poor. Michael does not have any emotional illness per se but clearly does have a very severe mixed personality disorder. There were no signs of a thought disorder. Michael's parenting abilities are appreciably, adversely impacted by his personality problems. It is likely that the women in his life have been far more important in Maria's parenting and values than has Michael.

My previous interaction with Michael, including the situation where he misreported what I told him about making financial arrangements for the evaluation is already part of the record and will not be repeated here. I asked Michael to fill out a registration and release of information form and Michael refused to do so. He indicated that he had done so previously and had a copy of it and sent a copy to his attorney. In fact, my secretary checked through the chart and was unable to locate such a form. I told that to Michael and he continued to refuse to sign it. After ten minutes of interviewing, Michael said that he would fill out the form at the end of the session. This is but one example of passive-aggressive behavior. Therefore, it was almost laughable when Michael said, "I'm not trying to be noncompliant."

When asked what he thought was the purpose for this session Michael said, "It's a psychiatric evaluation, I presume to determine my fitness as a parent and human being, as the father of Maria."

When asked how he thought Maria was doing, Michael said, "I think she's doing fine." When asked what specific problems he was concerned about in Maria, he said, "I'm concerned about my ability to motivate her in school." He then said, "I think we have that under control now." Things have been brought under control through the cooperation "from people who have been inspirational" to Maria, namely those members of his family who have been successful. When asked about the school problems, Michael said that she is now starting to "feel her oats as a young lady." Maria has achieved a level of success due to her personality and attractiveness and this has made her "very heady." As a result of that, the child has had trouble prioritizing her studies. He said that another problem which enters into the equation, and he is not sure of the weight of this problem, is that "she doesn't take tests well." When asked if there were any other problems that he is concerned about with Maria, Michael said, "this case has her unsettled . . . there's some anger." Otherwise, Maria does not have any problems.

When asked how many times he has been married, Michael said, "legally?" He said that he has been married legally three times and non-legally "about five." When asked how that came about he said, "Let's take Sofia, the police were looking for me due to a former partner." (This was an example of Michael's blaming someone else for his misfortune.) He said that he married Sofia because he believed that Maria would have a secure environment there, but sadly learned that Sofia was not the person to provide such an environment.

When asked about the other nonlegal marriage, Michael said that it was with Gayle Higgins because, "I fell in love with Gayle. . . she demanded marriage." He said that he knew that his other divorce was in the works and, "I was really [up in the air] at the time because I had a lot of problems. . . disregarded my own better judgment." After the session was over Michael returned to make a couple of further remarks, one of which was that the legal case that drained his finances, strained his relationship with Gayle and led to this separation. Gayle indicated in her deposition material that was quite to the contrary. I would tend to question Michael's reliability without having interviewed Gayle.

Michael's first legal marriage was to Anna and they broke up. Four kids resulted from that union. The breakup was due to "a terrible mistake in judgment . . . I slept with Jennifer one night on my boat" and Jennifer became pregnant. He said that there were other factors that troubled them including problems with the IRS. Michael also was experiencing serious problems with a very large job in the real estate area. He was a developer, architect, etc. and committed a great many of his personal assets to the project. The son-in-law of the president of the client cooperation absconded with some money and the company went out of business. Michael took a financial bath as a result of that. When asked how he got along with his four kids Michael said, "Today, excellent." When asked what that meant since it appeared today was a qualifier Michael said, "One of the good things that's come out of this custody crap . . . they've practically closed in with us." In the past his relationship with his kids was "arms length, friendly, loving but preoccupied with their own lives." Michael said that he really didn't push for more closeness in the relationship with his older kids.

Michael's second marriage was to Jennifer very shortly after his previous dissolution. He explained, Jennifer became pregnant, which induced him to marry her. Michael said that Anna stayed with him for nine months after Maria was born and was trying to work things out with him. He said that Anna was a "damn near perfect" wife and a "damn near perfect" mother. Then the affair occurred and "Anna couldn't handle the publicity" because Michael was a high profile individual. When asked how long he and Jennifer had been together, Michael said, "I don't remember" other than it was sporadic. Michael set Jennifer up in a home with a pool, provided money for her and partially furnished the home. He said that he visited Maria there. However, "later I couldn't afford that." When asked for further information about the relationship with Jennifer, Michael said, "I've blanked on a lot of it." I obtained the impression that Michael really didn't want to answer questions about the relationship with Jennifer because perhaps Jennifer would be able to disprove some of what he told me or it might look bad for him based on true answers.

Michael's third marriage was to Alicia McNeal. It lasted only six years. When asked why it broke up he said, "Oh boy.

. . no real valid reasons as we concluded recently." He said that at times her family interfered but overall, "it was wonderful." Michael described Alicia as being very different from Anna but nonetheless a great wife.

Michael's education included graduate schools, after two years in the navy, he spent two years at the University of Texas where he obtained a Master's in Business Administration. He previously had a Bachelor's Degree in Business Administration from the University of Colorado, and had taken classes at Wharton Business School. Michael also took Naval Sciences when he was in the navy. He said that he qualified for graduation, but the navy moved him out before he could complete his degree in Naval Sciences.

When asked how good a student he had been Michael said that he was a lousy high school student and amended this to "slightly above average." He especially enjoyed math and the sciences. Michael said that he had no trouble understanding the work but that he was most often indifferent. However, "In the navy I was considered pretty brilliant." Michael never had any academic or behavioral difficulties. He attended high school in Texas. Michael got along with his teachers "superbly" and when asked about his peer relationship he said, "we're still close." Michael said that he had five very, very close friends, two of whom are deceased. One of his friends dates back to grade school.

Michael currently works in "two locations . . . one menial." He is a janitor at the Evergreen Club where he does maintenance and other work approximately twenty-eight hours per week. He has been at this job for four months. He is also an assistant to a close friend in the marine services business and manages wealthy people's boats. Michael has been doing this since 1990 and he said that his hours are quite variable but average about twenty-five hours per week.

Prior to his current employment Michael worked in a similar marine services business with his friend and is working on being a Mate and a Master. Prior to that time he was unemployed but, "I can't remember the dates" that he was unemployed. I do not trust Michael's memory in that regard. Prior to that time, he was working through work release and the Berk County jail. I decided to not push for further information about Michael's work history.

His most important job was "my own business." He was the Chief Executive Officer for five small to midsize companies that provided architectural and engineering and other services. He had these businesses for about fifteen years. Michael said that one particular project "brought me down." It involved a sum of money and the son-in-law of the president of the client company.

According to Michael he was in the navy from the age of sixteen until twenty-two. He was in a submarine service. They also did coastal patrols. Michael was discharged as a Lieutenant, Junior Grade and had an almost perfect record. When asked what the almost meant, he said that he washed out of aviation training for a rule violation when he flew a troubled plane back and had to make an emergency landing. He was also suspended for three days.

Michael has never so much as experimented with illicit drugs and there is no family history of such drug use.

When asked about his alcohol consumption, Michael said that he has about one beer a month. He denied any alcohol related problems despite having been picked up for three DWI's "when I was involved with Jennifer." This appeared to be another attempt to blame someone else, specifically Jennifer, for his problems. Michael said that he was only convicted on one DWI because on two occasions "my attorneys were able to work me out of them." He said that there was short term abuse of alcohol and that it lasted about one year because, "I didn't know how to handle it" due to lack of awareness. When asked whether there was any family history of alcohol related problems Michael said, "No, none, ever."

Michael has been arrested on four occasions. His first was related to an IRS violation. Michael paused and was obviously thinking a great deal before saying that he failed to pay his taxes for two years and was charged for alleged fraud. Seven out of ten charges were dropped. Michael pled guilty, was sentenced for two years, and spent thirteen months at the State Penitentiary.

Michael's second arrest was about ten years later when "my partnership erupted." He said that he was arrested for "misuse of the company credit card" to pay company bills. He said that this arrest was based on the company credit card having already been canceled. When asked whether he had made any personal charges on the credit card he said, "I might on a couple of small ones." He said that in effect he was cheated out of eighteen thousand dollars. Michael served six months in the Berk County jail in work release.

Michael's third arrest occurred when he was involved with Gayle and worried about Maria. He said, "I created a letter" which he subsequently tried to withdraw in court. He was convinced that the case was "mishandled by my attorney." Michael said that he didn't have the courage to stand up for himself and was charged with forgery. Extra time was added to his work release program and he served a total of six of nine months.

When asked about the fourth arrest, Michael said that it was for "allegedly shoplifting cigarettes." He explained that it was a farce, that he had witnesses and the charges were dismissed. This occurred about a year and one half ago.

Michael's mother, age ninety-four years, is frail of body and agile of mind. She has had two hip replacements. Michael's father died when Michael was eight years of age. He sustained injuries as a metallurgical mining engineer when he was caught in a premature blast. Michael said that his mother never remarried and he does not know why that was the case.

Michael recalled that his father, "was a loving guy" who was quite generous. He "seemed to be very well liked" and it made Michael feel good years later when people spoke positively about his father.

Michael had two half-sisters and a deceased half-brother that were the products of his father's previous marriages. The marriage to Michael's mother was the father's third marriage. Michael said that he had a "wonderful" relationship with his half-siblings when they were kids. The half-siblings lived with them because Jim's father's wife had died. He now gets along "terrific" with his sisters who live in Maine and Alabama.

When asked what it was like growing up in his family and his home, Michael said that he just has positive memories. His mother raised Michael's half-siblings after their father died. He said that it was "tough" after his sisters married and his brother became an attorney. They left the home and "I was left alone." It was a problem because "my mother was constantly ill." From twelve or thirteen years of age Michael took jobs in order to help the family. He said that he played football and received a scholarship to Texas Tech but chose to join the navy instead. He claimed that he joined the navy because war was expected and "thought we'd get a leg up" by going in early and choosing what they wanted to do. Michael said that he was a big guy and was believed to be seventeen years of age and did not correct the person.

Michael said that his mother was "very old fashioned" and had a very strict value system. Otherwise, they got along well when he was a child. He said that she was a devoted Catholic, "probably too devoted for my digestion." When asked about his relationship with his mother as an adult, Michael said, "my mother and I have the most wonderful relationship now." However, his mother is now much more secure than she was when Michael was younger and, therefore, the relationship is not as important to her.

When asked about his plans for the future, Michael spoke about being a Mate and a Master. He would also like to consult in management with his friend for boats of more than fifty-five feet in length. He wants to "be a good citizen, and a good father to Maria." Michael later came back to my office and said that he is planning to remarry Alicia because they both realize their mistake and have worked things out. Even if they don't remarry they will live together. It is my impression that Michael is totally dependent on a relationship with a woman for either emotional needs or financial needs.

When asked if there was anything that he wanted to add to this session, Michael really had nothing more to contribute. I told him that I needed to see Maria again and another appointment was scheduled.

Michael's MMPI-2 was totally consistent with the clinical evaluation. It noted his moderate defensiveness and his tendency toward giving socially correct answers and minimization of weaknesses. Indeed, the MMPI-2 picked up the passive-aggressive personality trends and the resentment of family members that are unforgiving, if not bitter. Michael's judgment appears uneven and there is plenty of historical data to indicate breakdowns of his impulse controls. Indeed, Michael attempted to maintain an outward manner of composure and imperturbability as if he were "on top of everything." Michael does tend to project his angry feelings and aggressive impulses onto others. He clearly expresses his anger in indirect and manipulative ways. I noted Michael's dependency needs. While the MMPI-2 did not specifically pickup antisocial personality traits, it did note passive-aggressive traits and the paranoid trends.

Diagnostic impression: DSM-III, Diagnosis 1) 301.90 Personality disorder mixed type (passive-aggressive and antisocial).

Michael does have major personality problems that have led to a succession of dysfunctional relationships and socially inappropriate actions. His behavior is an extremely poor model for a child who is going through the identity state of life.

I will be reinterviewing Maria DeLorenzo at the request of her mother. I believe that Michael's personality style is totally consistent with the statements made by his "ex-wife" Gayle Higgins. While Jennifer Surel may indeed have some emotional problems and troubled personality traits, they pale in severity in comparison with those of Michael. I strongly support unrestricted contact between Jennifer and Maria. If there is any indication that Michael is either passively, actively, or passive-aggressively interfering with such contact I would then recommend that a change in residential parent be implemented. I believe that Jennifer would be far more equitable in "sharing" Maria with Michael than would be Michael with Jennifer.

I recognize that joint counseling may be needed to help resolve some of the problems between mother and daughter, problems that to a significant extent have been created by the father. I will defer any further comments until the end of my reevaluation of Maria. If you have any further questions regarding this evaluation, report, conclusions or recommendations, please feel free to contact me.

Sincerely,
Dr. Harold Topping

♦

To me, perhaps the most interesting thing Dr. Topping included in his evaluation was the statement, "It is my impression that Michael is totally dependent on a relationship with a woman for either emotional needs or financial needs." Reading this, I felt better about my own judgment which echoed his.

In fact, I suddenly remembered that Michael's own mother had intimated the same conclusion to me nearly two years before. At the time, it took me completely by surprise because talking about Michael was a painful subject for her and one I avoided. He was her only child and a source of great shame.

After the shock of learning of Michael's bigamy, I cut back my visits to Michael's mother. But the times I did go I marveled that Grandma was beautiful despite her shrunken and frail body. She asked for Maria whenever I came to see her and I finally explained Michael and I no longer lived together. She was not surprised and spoke without reservation about their relationship and her feelings.

"It was unbearable for me when he was in prison," she said. "I was old and sick and he wrote to me complaining about his family, how they were all against him. He planned to write a book in retaliation. I told him, 'It's not your children's fault you are in prison, and it is high time to think of peace before you find yourself right back in there. Mark my words. The Tempter will not rest until you are back in there. You cut your nose off of your own face.' I knew everything he did, Sofia. I read it all in the newspapers. I know people in my church who have relatives in Portland. I read the clippings that they sent me and I was horrified. I almost died with grief and pain while he was in prison, and now he tells everyone how he looked out for my welfare." She shook her head in disbelief.

"Never did he take care of me. I earned my own money, and can't even count the money I funneled into his family. I never got a penny back and had to turn each penny around twice before I spent it. I begged him to do some righteous thinking, to think before making a decision. But he doesn't listen. Everyone knew me in my church, and everybody knows I did my best in bringing him up, but he went his own way."

My heart went out to her. Now I looked at Jennifer and saw in her face the same sadness I had seen in Michael's mother's. Her fear is for Maria's future. It is a valid fear. When children excel it is not by chance. A critical element is the example parents set before the children. A parent must make a tremendous investment. After that they must hope and pray it is enough to help formulate the beginning of real character. Ultimately, the choices both parents and children make, are their own. In the end people must take responsibility for themselves.

Years ago Michael chose his own way and it led him straight into the files of the Federal Bureau of Investigation.

*T*he depositions proceeded, as did the rest of the custody case, in fits and starts. Michael's major tactic seemed to be delays and sidetracks. This maneuver fit perfectly with the wheels of justice which ground so slowly as to make forward movement, at times, imperceptible. Nevertheless, we did move forward.

Anna, Michael's first wife, offered to testify if she was needed. Craig Walters deposed Alicia McNeal, who despite all Michael had done to her, still seemed half intoxicated, only half clear headed about her ex-husband. This was easily seen when she answered Craig Walters' questions. Walters, a sympathetic person, leaned toward Alicia as if he could hardly believe what she was saying.

"Anything else?"

Alicia shook her head, "No."

Walters continued probing, "You also suggest in the declaration that that may have been a mistake that ultimately has led to some of his current legal problems. How do you mean that?"

Alicia frowned, "Well, maybe he would not have made the choices that he's made since then, some not too wise, had we still been together."

"By his current legal problems, what are you referring to?" Walters asked.

She shook her head, "Probably his credit card thing and the bad checks, whatever that involved."

Walters took a deep breath, "Okay. Do you blame yourself for that?"

"No," Alicia said softly.

Walters stared at her. "The indication that I get from you, from several of your answers to questions, is that you feel that you had some emotional problems that you were going through at the time and after the time of your separation; is that correct?"

"Yes," Alicia replied.

"What was the cause of those?"

"Probably many factors."

"Such as?"

She hesitated then spoke. "Well, we were having some real financial problems. That's probably the biggest one."

"What was the source of your financial problems?" Walters asked.

"There wasn't any money."

"There wasn't any money?" he repeated shaking his head.

"Right," she nodded.

"Your inheritance or whatever, the money that you had received as a result of your prior husband's death, was gone at that point?"

"Right," Alicia looked away.

"You weren't working?"

"No."

"Was Mr. DeLorenzo working?"

"Right."

"Pardon?"

"Yes."

Walters wanted to draw out more of Alicia's present attitude and current relationship with Michael DeLorenzo. "My understanding is that your contact with Mr. DeLorenzo," he paused, "since your separation has been pretty regular?"

"Well, what's regular?" Alicia asked slowly.

"Once or twice a week?"

She nodded, "I may talk to him. I don't see him that often."

"But you're in some kind of communication?"

"Right. Particularly when it comes to the custody thing with Maria."

"But he has never told you anything about filing bankruptcy?"

"No," Alicia looked distinctly uncomfortable now.

Her discomfort grew as Craig Walters began to delve deeper into Alicia's perceptions of Jennifer. From her answers, it was evident that Alicia had gleaned all her information and beliefs from Michael DeLorenzo. To me, her words merely echoed Michael's and I felt that she still accepted all the things about Jennifer as the real truth. At the same time, I felt reality had begun to confront her and penetrate the barrier Michael had erected. For instance, Alicia's feelings of fear were discernible when Craig Walters asked her:

"Based on your filing of the [first] protection order, is it fair to assume that you took that to mean that he might harm you physically?"

Alicia slowly replied, "I—probably in that state of mind was thinking that, yes." She frowned.

However, immediately afterward, Alicia conveyed the feelings of attraction which still tied her to Michael DeLorenzo.

"You make mention in your declaration that the dissolution of your marriage to Mr. DeLorenzo may have been a mistake. What do you mean by that?"

Alicia flushed. "Well, we still probably care for one another."

As I saw it, this self-imposed veil, "the willing suspension of disbelief" which seemed to always occur in Michael's relationships had already been lifted from the perceptions of the other women who had been among the wives of Michael DeLorenzo.

This was clearly discernible in Gayle Higgins' testimony. A year or so before, she had, like Alicia, accepted Michael's beliefs and made them her own. The depths of these shared beliefs she illustrated, at that time, in a letter to the Court:

I am Gayle M. DeLorenzo, wife of Michael DeLorenzo, stepmother of Maria DeLorenzo.

After reading Jennifer Surel's declaration which was full of untrue accusations and so many untruths Jennifer fabricated, I had to respond. My declaration is to state the true facts not only as Maria's stepmother but as a woman of integrity and high moral values. So, to not waste my time or the Court's on rebuttal of all petitioner's gibberish, I'll get right to the heart of the matter, my one and only concern: Maria DeLorenzo.

First, Maria is very well taken care of and loved deeply, sincerely, by her father, Michael, and I, which she is very well aware of. Maria and I met when she was 12 years of age, and from that first moment we both felt a special bond between us. It was everything good and beautiful, as if the good Lord was saying this will be her home, she belongs here with me and Michael.

Becoming her mother was as easy and natural as if I had given birth to her. I wanted to be her mother, to love her, care for her whether she was ill or well, protecting her, being her best friend, giving her a stable Christian home and the love and friendship of my own living child; and, of course, reprimanding and disciplining her when needed as I have done with my own family. Maria has blossomed under my/our care.

She did not need months of knowing me to accept me as her mother. Does a duck take to water? That is how it was with Maria and me.

Last Christmas I wrote in Maria's card, which she can confirm: "Honey, the most beautiful gift you can give me is the day you feel comfortable to call me mom." Within two weeks she referred to me as mom, but not expecting it so soon I didn't hear it. She came to me and wondered why I didn't respond. I told her, and then we hugged and, of course, I cried, and since then I have been Mom or Mother, and we both want it to continue as it has been. My point is that love is not something—exactly, that, and much more to destroy our daughter's life. Love and wanting to be with someone is a free choice. Maria has taken the choice freely. She has a good healthy mind. She is 14-1/2 years of age now. She is not the small child that Jennifer and her attorney keep referring to.

Just because Jennifer is Maria's biological mother does not earn Jennifer this right.

Jennifer must understand that if she truly knows the meaning of a mother's love. I would like someone in Family Court to ask Jennifer what her definition of love is, because so far I haven't seen this great so-called mother's love she declares in her declarations.

Jennifer's love is destructive and self-serving. Jennifer's approach from the beginning was not with any sincerity regarding Maria. It was only to hurt and try to destroy Maria's father. Going through Maria is just a ploy. Her unethical tactics, her unnecessary methods, private investigator, prying into my personal life, lies, declarations from sources that distort the truth—trying to destroy the man Maria loves and respects deeply, as I do; the psychiatric evaluation that was approved by the Court but instigated by Jennifer and Mr. Walters—which should never have been considered if she had any love for Maria. Did she ever even stop to think of how this effected Maria? Is this the only way she can show love? Is this love? No, it is not! Again, she is hurting Maria. Maria resents having to be evaluated; in fact, Maria resents Jennifer's whole intrusion into her life. Jennifer and/or her attorney either realize this fact or just do not want to admit Jennifer's failure.

Now, because of the enormous unpaid attorney's fees incurred by Mr. Walters' client, they make this motion and included an order for payment, continuing to harass us.

Jennifer has nothing to lose because she started with nothing, apparently, has nothing, which I still cannot understand for if she was constantly employed in a respectable position, saved money, established a stable residence within the ten-year period of time she would have quite enough to pay her attorney's fees and more, rather than coming with an empty purse to expensive legal action instead of a different approach, and now expecting us to cover her expensive legal actions. No! That should be her total responsibility! We have our own serious problems with money at this time. Jennifer has had only herself to take care of; what did she do with her income? Just because she is the biological mother of Maria, does that mean we have to cover her debts? No? That should be her own problem, just as we have our own!

In Jennifer's declarations she continually states that Michael and I have influenced Maria against her. We/I have never discouraged or tried to think for Maria regarding her biological mother. This is where I stand regarding our daughter and my husband, I will do it with my head held high.

To sum it all up, Jennifer wants all of the roses in the garden but none of the thorns. Roses come with thorns.

I certify under penalty of perjury under the laws of the State of Oregon that the foregoing is true.

Gayle H. DeLorenzo

Yet, less than a year later, Gayle's ideas about Michael, Maria, and Jennifer Surel had changed drastically. Now she testified:

"You and Jennifer, as far as I was concerned, were my enemies. Okay? And that resulted—because I loved my husband at the time, I believed in him totally, I could never—and when I met Mr. DeLorenzo, what he told me about Jennifer, I believed him. I believed everything he told me at that point in time. So I—of course, I went and I thought, 'Hey, why should someone get into my—' I'm a private person, and I thought, 'why should this woman—' this is my thought then, 'Why should I divulge my personal, my financial? She has no business to it.' Because I thought she was these terrible things, that he told me."

Craig asked, "What did he tell you? [about Jennifer Surel]."

"Unfit mother. She had a violent temper."

Walters broke in, "Did he . . ."

Gayle nodded. "Cheated, lied."

"Excuse me."

"Cheated, lied, stole. I didn't hear one good thing about Jennifer."

"Were any or all of these things told to you in front of Maria?"

She sighed heavily, "Some of them, yes."

"Was it in fact—" Walters tried to edge in but Gayle's answer poured out in a stream-of-consciousness flow.

"And I became part of it. I became part. I did too. I'm not going to deny I did not."

"What do you mean by, 'you became part of it'? How did you become part of it?"

"By involving myself in believing him, that I believed, and—you know, and when I saw Jennifer, I saw her differently. When you're told that someone is no good, you look at them and that's how you see them. Stereotype people."

Gayle went on. "Yes," she said softly, then her voice rose. "Obviously you stereotype people when somebody tells you about someone. But I look at her differently now. . . . And I do believe that Jennifer Surel does love Maria. That, I believe. I am a woman and I'm a mother. Now when I see her, in a different way, she is not my friend, best friend or anything like that. She is an acquaintance. But I believe she loves her daughter, and she will not harm Maria. And I believe they should have the visitation. I believe that Maria has been brainwashed. I have—I was, and I'm an adult, a mature, intelligent woman. Because Maria has been taught to lie. She kept the truth from me, but little by little, some of the truths came out."

"What do you mean she's been taught to lie?" Craig asked.

As the subject turned to Maria, more information about the torn girl surfaced.

"Maria kept the truth from me, and I think it hurt her."

"Which truth?"

"There's a lot of things inside of Maria that need to come out. And I think Mr. Hadon should be aware of it, and so should Dr. Topping because she's a very young girl. There's a lot of anger inside of her, and I think it's very unfair for a parent to put a very young child in that position. It's a lot of burden. It really is."

"How was she put in that position?" Walters was obviously looking for a specific answer referring to Michael and the ill effects he had on his daughter.

"By Mr. DeLorenzo telling her. Basically, he speaks for her a tremendous amount of the time, and Maria does not like that. And by just having her suppress the truth. How do you expect her to grow up, she's going to be a mother one day, if she's taught not to tell the truth now?"

Later Gayle spoke about how she had slowly learned, despite her wish not to, of Michael DeLorenzo's duplicity.

"We were married, if you want to call it married, February 14th. In March he went ahead and applied for credit cards. And the credit cards he applied for were Chase Manhattan Visa, Chase Manhattan Advantage, First Card, Mileage Plus. He took out Exxon, he took out Chevron, Discover. And he went ahead—which I have them here, I've got some of them, and put me down as the applicant." Gail reflected for a moment.

"I know now, as I'm telling you this, but at the time I wasn't aware that he put me down as the applicant. And all this information is incorrect, and he forged my name. Okay? And all the information is incorrect. In fact, he even put my mother's maiden name incorrect, and he put me as if I was an investor, secretary-treasurer with Allied Group, what have you, and he used my name, Higgins. He did it because, at that point in time, he was still married to Sofia. He was [also] married to Alicia McNeal, without my knowledge. As I'm talking, I'll explain again, I wasn't aware of any of this. He needed funds for the annulment regarding Sofia, he needed money, I assume now, as I read his letter, to pay Alicia, and debts. So when he applied for these cards, he used the name Gayle Higgins. Because my credit history was excellent," Gayle went on to explain the details of some of Michael's deceptions.

"What Mr. DeLorenzo would—was doing in the past was, he would—he had checks made up, and at first I wasn't aware of them until all of a sudden the checks were bouncing or returned 'Not Sufficient Funds.' Let's call them NSF's. Or else there were times he would take them from my purse and he would take them from the back of the checks, and I wasn't aware until all of a sudden I was—the sequence was incorrect, or I would get calls from the bank. And at one point in time he took the checks from—you know, how you get them in your little group, and—but he said that I called it stealing and he denied it, he did not call it stealing. He said, you know that 'I'm your husband, this is a normal thing,' and to me it's not. You just don't do that. I'm an honest and aboveboard person, and so I did close it. I wanted to protect—It wasn't his money, that was my money."

Walters asked a further question. "So he would take checks out of your purse?"

"At times he had taken checks out of my purse."

"Did you take steps to avoid having that happen?"

"He said he would never do it again, and you know, I believed him. And then he promised that he wouldn't—if he writes checks that I would like him to tell me, because I kept track of the checkbook."

She added the postscript:

"And there were times that my mortgage payment would come back."

Gayle explained the lies which had brought her over the edge.

"And when I went to Florida, I was gone a week, and he was—told me he was flown down by Mr. Dodenberg by helicopter to review this resort. I talked to Mr. Dodenberg, and he didn't fly Michael down. In fact, he hasn't spoken with Mr. DeLorenzo for quite a while."

She took a deep breath and went on. "Then there was another job, the Ryan job, back in Springfield, Illinois. His name is Mr. Olin. He had met with Mr. Ryan in Portland one evening—not with Mr. Ryan, strike that please—Mr. Olin and Catherine Post Richards. And they met in person. I called Mr. Olin myself, and when I got him on the phone, he thought I was crazy. And I said, 'Mr. Olin, I understand your position,' I said, 'but I'm calling because I want to protect my investment.' That's basically when he made a statement that he never was in Portland, he never met Catherine Post Richards. He had spoken with Mr.

DeLorenzo on the telephone because Mr. DeLorenzo requested some information, and that's all. And when I confronted Mr. DeLorenzo about him meeting Mr. Olin, he said, 'No, flesh to flesh.'"

"What do you mean? I don't understand," Walters said.

"That's what Mr. DeLorenzo said, 'No, we met flesh to flesh.' That was his statement."

"In other words, Mr. Olin had been lying to you?"

"I don't believe Mr. Olin would lie to me. He had no reason to lie."

"How did you track Mr. Olin down?"

"Mr. DeLorenzo gave misinformation, and there are things he has mentioned to me and they have slipped my mind. But I'm not that stupid of a woman. Some things began to stick to me."

Walters probed deeper into Gayle's final reason for divorcing Michael DeLorenzo.

"Was your money going to fund the custody litigation?"

"No, but that was part—No, I didn't say that. But that's part of the reason why we weren't getting funds, was because of the custody litigation." She paused, looked into Walters' eyes, the depth of her feelings rising up and told him, "I had nothing else to give him. I just lost my fight, okay, I gave up."

Walters nodded sympathetically. "Okay. You've read Mr. DeLorenzo's recent declaration with the nine page letter to Mr. Hadon that you've referred to here. Is it your reading of that, that he portrays that it was the litigation that was the sole cause of your relationship breaking up?"

"Yes. That's what I..."

Walters broke in, "Do you agree with that?"

"No. No," Gayle said vehemently.

"Can you just briefly tell me why you disagree with that?"

Emotion brimming, Gayle, her voice halting, responded, "It wasn't just the litigation. It was the fact that I knew that he used me the whole time. He never loved me, he used me from day one, and all of a sudden it clicked with me. Okay?" She stopped to take a deep breath of air and went on. "And I was devastated by that because I gave my all. And I, just at that point in time, thought to myself what a fool I was."

As the depositions continued, I began to wonder why Craig Walters didn't question Michael DeLorenzo. I told myself that Craig knew what he was doing but finally, just as the last of the depositions were drawing to a close, I couldn't help asking him. Craig threw back his head laughing heartily. When he stopped, he replied, "Why the hell should I? He'd only tell more lies. Let him save them for the trial."

◆

Finally all the depositions were over. Last minute preparations were made as we anxiously awaited the actual trial.

It was a long wait. First, Michael's counsel broke his leg and the court date was postponed. A new one was set for March 11. This too was postponed, and another one scheduled for April Fool's Day. The date was fitting, I chuckled, but before long it, too, was discarded and still another one, May 6, was chosen. This one seemed to hold.

Jennifer's stress lessened, I felt relieved and began to concentrate on putting my own work and personal life in order. I was dating again. The weekend was to be a busy one.

Friday, three days before the trial, I was busily running errands. A quick stop to deposit a paycheck immediately rearranged my priorities.

As I whipped into a parking space at Atlantic-First Bank I was startled to see Michael DeLorenzo standing directly in front of me. He was frantically searching in his wallet for something. Two things flew through my mind; he hasn't yet seen me, and I don't have a gun with me. Knowing he'd seen the list of witnesses slated to testify against him, and was aware I was on it, I quickly backed out of the parking slot. I then parked in a less exposed area watching him all the time. He used the cash machine located on the outside wall of the bank, then carefully studied the receipt an unusual length of time. This piqued my curiosity.

I leaned forward to get a better look and saw him wander slowly back to a parked Cadillac. Absentmindedly, he reached out his hand to the car door. Suddenly, he pulled back, apparently realizing it was not his automobile. He walked a few more paces and got into a new Toyota Nissan. Getting out of the car, I ran to a spot where I could get a good look at the license number. I peered at Michael through the window of a parked car. Suddenly, I realized how very odd I might appear to an onlooker, and began to laugh at myself.

Odd or not, I still memorized the plate letters and numbers. I jotted them down on some scratch paper when I returned to my car, then watched as Michael drove away. As soon as he was gone I rushed into the bank and spoke with the Assistant Manager. I quickly ran through Michael's more recent criminal background. "I am concerned that he has recently been in the company of an unknown woman. My main fear is that Michael may have gained access to her bank account through the cash machine." The manager was polite and attentive, took some notes and thanked me for my concern.

I returned home as quickly as I could and made several telephone calls. The first was to Jennifer Surel. I told her what I'd witnessed and gave her the license number.

"I'm swamped. Could you call Craig?" she asked. Just before she hung up she whispered, "I'll love you forever for this!"

I called Craig Walters' office to give him the license number and car description. I asked him to access the information. Then I called the Head of Operations at the Hillsdale Police Department and reported that I had just seen Michael DeLorenzo, and gave him the license number. I repeated the information for the Silverrock Police Department Commander five minutes later. Finally, feeling I had covered all bases, I sat down to await a call back. It took longer than I anticipated, nearly twenty-four hours.

When the phone finally rang, it was Craig. "The car is registered to a Ms. Cindy Emery, recent divorcee. I remember the case, her divorce was finalized last summer. She received a large settlement, approximately two hundred thousand dollars," Craig explained.

He went on, "She received $72,000 in July or August and $132,000 in October. Michael moved in mid-October or the first of November."

"Damn," was my immediate response, then I added, "Michael only lived with Gayle two days before he applied for the first credit card in her name. He's been living with Cindy for six months." I paused thinking out loud. "Among all the other things she'll lose, she has no concept of the jeopardy her finances are in."

When I told Jennifer, she asked, "Do you think the Hillsdale Police Department will warn her?"

I sighed. "I don't know. They didn't warn Gayle when I went to them, but you never know. When I called this time I had a better response. I'm going to call them back in a few minutes and let them know about the settlement. The more information they have the better."

◆

As the trial's zero hour approached, nerves became tighter and tighter. Fear was added to my own agitation when an intruder was sighted several times at my place of work. In addition, twice when the workday ended I walked out to my car and found the windows broken. By then I was just plain scared. I applied for and received a permit to carry a concealed weapon. I didn't like doing it, but I knew I might need to protect myself. I encouraged Jennifer to do the same when we next saw each other.

In that meeting we also discussed the future and Jennifer's present feelings.

Jennifer's dilemma centered on Maria, who was now telling Jennifer that if she didn't drop the suit, Maria would never see her again. Jennifer was torn between telling the truth and doing what was right, or being loved. "I find it easier to face Michael's devastating lies than to face the quiet rejection implicit in Maria's demands to drop the suit," Jennifer said.

"I like to think that something good will come out of this tragedy, as monstrous and terrible as it is. The alternative is unthinkable," Jennifer replied almost as a prayer. "If one woman can learn from my mistakes and suffering, if one child can remain with her mother, perhaps it will be enough. I find, having survived it, I have more sympathy for others in destructive relationships, even ones I don't understand. It's taught me so much."

She was on the right track. "The learning for us both as well as the other women Michael has manipulated and deceived is far from over. The final lesson we have to learn is whether to move forward to love or not based on present realities, and not the past," I said earnestly to her. I knew that for Jennifer that would be very difficult. Yet, if she and Maria were to have a relationship again, it couldn't be based on what they had in Colorado. It has to spring from who they are now. I doubted she would get custody because of Maria's strong feelings. Yet I knew Jennifer was clinging to hope.

"Truth rarely arrives without a price," I offered.

Jennifer nodded, "There were two events that delivered invaluable information about motherhood to me: I lost my innocence about expert opinions by experiencing the Colorado justice system. Ultimately you stand alone, and your own instincts are the only safe ground to stand upon—only your own opinions are defendable. The second event was the wrenching goodbye with Maria when my nest emptied abruptly years before I expected. The separation I had to withstand, made me a better mother than I believed I could be. I recognized what a gift a child truly was and how temporal. They are truly God's little visitors in our homes. I knew that Maria's happiness depended on her independence. I had been given six years to teach her about love. I had to trust that she could remember, and endure."

Tears rose to my eyes. "Jennifer," I said softly, "I pray your trust is rewarded, if not in the way you seek by some other fulfilling answer."

Jennifer was silent.

The first day of the custody trial finally arrived. As we walked into the huge, chandelier lit courtroom I could feel Jennifer trembling next to me. She was scared but hopeful. As for me, I was determined to set the record straight for all of Michael's victims when I took the stand.

Craig Walters, Jennifer's attorney, briefed me on how the case would proceed. Basically, Craig was going to begin by showing the court Michael DeLorenzo's instability proved by the sheer numbers of homes he'd lived in, credit history replete with repossessions, evictions, defaults and lawsuits. It was a clever opening and not at all what the opposition would expect.

From there, Craig would move to Michael's marriages and bigamy.

My testimony was penciled in for the next morning. I took Jennifer to lunch at a small cafe near the court. When we returned, a slender, attractive woman with auburn hair was sitting in the gallery just behind Craig Walters. It was Gayle Higgins. She was scheduled to follow my testimony but Craig had called her to the stand immediately.

She adjusted the microphone and Craig began to ask her questions about Michael DeLorenzo. Her testimony was more muted than in the deposition but nevertheless, she laid the facts before us.

"Maria talked about all the places in Bermuda where she and Michael had been . . . I gave her more than I gave my own children.

I felt used by Michael. I feel used now, by Maria. They betrayed me. . . shortly before they left I noticed that she looked depressed. I asked her to talk to me. That's what a mother is for. Maria replied, 'You'll never know what I have bottled up inside me. I can't tell you.' I was sure that was horribly true."

When Craig Walters asked questions about their finances, Gayle clearly stated, "We lived on my money, my savings and checking account. I bought Mr. DeLorenzo a Cadillac. He left me with a lot of debts. My resources are down to nothing."

I could tell that in the time between the depositions and trial her perceptions of the truth about Michael DeLorenzo had further crystallized.

Gayle continued, "Until I discovered the credit . . . Yes, I can identify the applications for the credit cards. The signature is a forgery. I was paying for the support and also Hadon's fees. When I learned I wasn't legally married to Michael, Hadon suggested a divorce, but he said he would not handle it. I was very upset and angry. I cried. Maria finally told me she'd never been to Bermuda. He doesn't own a home in the Padgett section. I asked her why she didn't warn me. I could have gone to work, maybe the marriage would have worked..."

Craig Walters asked Gayle if Maria had ever mentioned Sofia.

"She never wanted me to know. She didn't want to hurt me. She kept things from me. She kept the statements from my bank. Once she gave them to me and Michael punished her . . . said she betrayed him . . . I don't blame her so much, when you're told things for years you believe it. If you take a child and tell them the same thing for years they'll believe. We had a wonderful rapport but she's made no effort to contact me," Gayle said sadly. She had now not only lost her own daughter to a drunk driver, but now had lost Maria as well.

"Have you heard of any other person who acted as a parent to her that has had contact?" Craig asked.

"No." She shook her head. "It wasn't encouraged. Michael opposed all visitation with Jennifer, and I was guilty of putting words in Maria's mouth. I had encouraged Maria to give Jennifer the cold shoulder. I believed the lies that Michael told about Jennifer, I believed Michael was the nice person he presented himself to be. . . I lied in affidavits, but I believed at the time the statements were true."

As she admitted the mistakes of judgment she had made, Gayle's composure was exceptional. During the break I leaned forward to say earnestly, "I commend you on your courage."

"It's very difficult. If I had money I'd prosecute," she said.

"It doesn't take money to prosecute," I replied.

Gayle shook her head and sighed. "I want my life to go on. My real regret is the effects it's had on Maria. I'm afraid of what it's going to do to Maria when she is an adult. I'd like to see Maria again, maybe hear a thank you for what I've done for her—I was used—hits you in the gut, being used . . . and here he is today as Mr. Wonderful DeLorenzo. It stinks."

Craig Walters was strong and bold, a better attorney than I had anticipated. Byron Hadon who was known for his powerful interrogations was almost retiring. Perhaps he now recognized the truth and didn't want to dispute it by manipulation. As the women Michael had hurt so badly and the other witnesses departed the stand with only token challenge to their testimony, their words left an indelible picture of Michael DeLorenzo's dishonest and debased character. It became increasingly obvious to me that Michael and his attorney would have to rest their entire case on Maria's fragile shoulders. The years of manipulation and control were to be put to the supreme test.

When it was my turn, I was determined, despite my nervousness, not to leave anything out. I wanted to tell the judge all about the pain and harm Michael DeLorenzo had inflicted on my life as well as on so many others.

In answer to Craig's first question about how I met Michael, I told him, "I met Michael DeLorenzo approximately four years ago. We began dating and Michael began telling me things about his life. He told me that he was in business with a partner. He said he had a home in Bermuda where he had traveled on his private plane, boated, and gone on sports car rides with his movie star friends."

Craig then let me freely tell my experiences and I spoke about nearly the same things as I had in my deposition. I repeated that I knew that he had been married three times before. As far as I could tell he had no contact with the children of his first marriage. And that he told me that he hated Alicia McNeal's son.

"From the beginning of our relationship I knew that he had a daughter, Maria. He told me that she lived with his business partner-paramour, a multimillionaire named Catherine Richards. He told me that Maria had a tutor who lived at the mansion and that the tutor traveled with them when they went to Bermuda and other places and that was why Maria was not going to school.""

I continued, "When I met Maria for the first time she confirmed to me the stories about her living in a mansion, having a tutor, the home in Bermuda, movie star connections and other such things that her father had told me. Mr. DeLorenzo and I decided to get 'married.' Put the word married in quotes because, entirely unknown to me, Mr. DeLorenzo was still married to Alicia McNeal.

"In conversations that I had with Maria before our wedding, Maria asked if she could come live with her father and me after we were married. I was surprised that she asked that because of all the wonderful things I had heard about the place she was supposedly living. I did, however, agree that she could come live with me when her father did after the marriage ceremony.

"During the period of time immediately after our marriage ceremony we were planning an extended vacation trip. We planned to go to Bermuda and spend time at Mr. DeLorenzo's home there and then go on to various other places. We planned to be gone for quite a while so we decided to wait and move Maria's things into my home after we returned. We were very busy planning this trip. Eventually, however, Mr. DeLorenzo stated that he could not go because Maria's mother had somehow 'blocked'

Maria's passport, making it impossible for her to go. He said he needed to stay here and get that straightened out.

"It was, therefore, mid-September before we actually moved Maria's things to my home. It was then that I knew the stories about her care had been lies. I went with Mr. DeLorenzo and Maria to get her things. Instead of going to a mansion in a wealthy section, it was a low income housing complex in Portland. Maria's possessions consisted of a very cheap, old bedroom set, an old, broken desk, a television set with Nintendo games, and a few boxes. Those were the only things at that apartment. Since Mr. DeLorenzo had been living in my home for about three months at that time and had not moved any furniture into my home, it appeared to me that perhaps Maria's furniture had been all that was there. I did not confront Maria and her father about the obvious lies they had been telling me. There just was no point, as there could not have been any believable explanation.

"Mr. DeLorenzo told Maria over and over again that it was wrong to be disloyal to him and to not go along with his stories and that disloyalty hurt him deeply. He has convinced her that he is the only one in the world who truly loves her and he has not only made her his accomplice in his fabrications but has convinced her that she is responsible for his happiness. Mr. DeLorenzo was extremely possessive of Maria. He drove her home from school everyday, saying he was afraid that she would be kidnapped.

"Mr. DeLorenzo has told Maria that he has a twenty-one million dollar trust fund established for her when she reaches age twenty-one. He has convinced her that he is unable to take any money from it now due to the terms and conditions of the trust and due to the fact that several people are out to get his money and ruin him. He has told her that she just has to bear with him and go along with him and his stories, through the good times and the bad and that she will receive her reward for her loyalty when she reaches age twenty-one. He also has told her that he is going through all of the problems he is going through just for her and her future . . . Mr. DeLorenzo told Maria and me terrible things about

Maria's mother. . . I am sure that Maria did not receive anything of substance that her mother might have sent her and I doubt that Mr. DeLorenzo would admit to Maria's mother trying to contact Maria. I did talk to Maria some about her mother. She had some memories from Denver and said she sometimes thought about her mother but she did not really seem to know much about her.

"Two years ago, Mr. DeLorenzo was arrested by the Hillsdale police. He was at a public housing apartment and my car was parked in front. Using my registration, the police called to tell me about my car. They also informed me that Mr. DeLorenzo was still married to Alicia McNeal. They told me that when they arrested him in his apartment, it contained his typewriter and several blank letterheads of various individuals and organizations.

"It became clear to me that Mr. DeLorenzo was not who or what he said he was and I refused to allow him to continue residing in my home. Mr. DeLorenzo's arrest and information I subsequently learned, made some things that happened while we were together make sense. I did not know what he did with his time during the day while I was at work. I since learned that he intercepted mail coming to the home, threw away bills and past due notices. He edited my telephone answering machine to weed out references or calls regarding past due bills. He took my outgoing mail saying that he was going to mail it and threw the bills I was paying in the back of the car. Much of those were discovered when the Hillsdale police arrested him and about four months of my mail was in the trunk of my car at that time...

"He constantly pressured me to open joint bank accounts, commingle funds and transfer car and house titles into both names. He became annoyed when I continually refused to do any of these things. At one time, he became very annoyed when I resisted him opening a bank account in both of our names in the North Star Bank. When I told him that I would go to every bank to make sure that my name was not used on any of his accounts, he became very angry and warned me in very explicit terms to stay away from the banks in our area.

"After I told Mr. DeLorenzo he could no longer live in my home, he left Maria there for about a month. Maria was very upset with me for not allowing her father to live in my home. I explained to her the best I could that I simply could not allow someone who was married to someone else to live with me. At that time Maria and I had some long talks about her lying and her father's lying. I tried to explain to her that going along with his lies and stories is the same as lying herself. She cried, admitted that she had been lying and that she knew it was wrong but she was expected to support her dad and not be disloyal to him and that was just the way it was.

"During the month that Mr. DeLorenzo lived away from my home and Maria lived with me, I tried to find someone who would help Maria. I called Ogdon Leeds, the only one of Mr. DeLorenzo's friends that I ever met. He suggested that I call Mr. DeLorenzo's son from his first marriage. I did that but he was not interested in helping with Maria and made it clear that he did not want anything to do with Mr. DeLorenzo and that I shouldn't either. He was not, however, able to provide any assistance regarding Maria.

"About a month after he left my home, Mr. DeLorenzo came and got Maria one day while I was at work. I insisted that Mr. DeLorenzo pay to have our marriage declared invalid. He hired Byron Hadon to do that. I had several conversations with Mr. Hadon and he told me he was aware that Mr. DeLorenzo is a liar and to be careful about believing what he says."

◆

When my testimony was over, I walked outside feeling better. I had done what I could.

Later, Joyce Solimine was seated on a long bench located outside the courtroom where she was scheduled to testify. Michael DeLorenzo approached Joyce, who was the widow of his former business associate, Alex. He bent to speak, then almost immediately left her and went into the courtroom where his attorney was waiting. Jennifer followed, seating herself at the adversarial table.

Within minutes, there was a brief exchange between the court clerk and Michael. He had turned his chair and now was facing the door to the judge's chamber. Tears were streaming down his face. The clerk, accustomed to courtroom melodrama, rolled her eyes and returned to her work.

An hour later, when Jennifer had completed her own time on the witness stand, it was up to the other witnesses to corroborate what she had told the court.

As court reconvened, Joyce Solimine walked to the stand. Once sworn in, she began answering the questions presented to her. As she talked, a clearer picture of Michael's work background and the complicated relationship between he and Alex Solimine surfaced. Though Joyce stated she had never liked or trusted Mr. DeLorenzo, she had been a dutiful wife and acquiesced to her husband's stated intention to "help" Michael after he got out of prison.

Craig Walters wanted the rest of the story. "Prior to Michael's serving time in the penitentiary, were there any business deals involving your husband and Michael DeLorenzo?"

Joyce replied, "When Mr. DeLorenzo was faced with the IRS problem, he told Alex that the IRS wanted money and he wanted his help in putting together a sale of some property. Alex tried to put together a package deal, but there was some question on one of the properties and the attorney for the buyer just simply said 'no.'

"After Mr. DeLorenzo went to prison, my husband always felt very guilty. He felt if the deal had gone through, it would have been all right."

Craig asked, "Do you have an opinion as to whether that influenced your husband's later decision to involve himself in business with Mr. DeLorenzo?"

"I'm sure it did." Joyce nodded. "I think Mr. DeLorenzo played on that guilt. In the last year of my husband's life, I could have had the satisfaction of telling him, 'I told you so,' but I never did. He realized he had been had, and how he had been had. He really didn't believe anything anymore."

Craig led her in another direction. "Let's go into a little more detail now about how it happened that your husband set up the company that Michael was involved in."

She nodded. "Michael was trying to work, as I understood it, as a developer. My husband told him that if he got his real estate license they could go into business. But he never got it. He did do a lot of typing, he was very good at that, and he answered the telephones. My husband felt that in order for Michael to get back on his feet, he needed a platform from which to work."

Despite her husband's good intentions, the situation deteriorated. Joyce explained, "Well, my husband had given Michael an ultimatum. He was to start contributing or my husband was not going to renew the lease on the office space. Mr. DeLorenzo had some very elaborate plans and he decided to lease the office space across the hallway for a company he was going to start. When we closed our office, Michael had all our telephones moved across the hall. I went home and asked my husband, 'Are the telephones still in your name?' He said, 'well, yeah.' He had credit with the telephone company and Mr. DeLorenzo didn't. He ended up paying over four hundred dollars to the phone company because Michael had moved those phones without his knowledge.

"My husband closed the office. He was a broken man emotionally. He had been through a lot in those ten years. He was then diagnosed with cancer. Two years later, he died."

While Joyce spoke, Michael showed no emotion at all. He never looked at his ex-partner's wife. Instead he gazed straight ahead.

Craig's attention, however, didn't waiver. "So initially, Michael DeLorenzo was to obtain a real estate license and be an agent in this operation?"

Joyce sighed. "He was to be a developer. He had the knowledge to be a developer but without the real estate license. . . I understand that a broker can't take just anyone."

Craig said, "He was to get that license but never did, yet he stayed in that business relationship for ten years. Is that correct?"

Joyce murmured, "Yes."

Craig went on. "What did he do?"

"He made a lot of phone calls." Joyce replied in a quiet bitter voice. "Sent out packages by Federal Express and did advertising. I saw the bills when they came in. Mainly, I think it was a lot of 'busy work.'"

Craig nodded. "Were you there when deals closed? Were you aware who was responsible for those deals? What was the percentage of deals from your husband and what percentage were from Mr. DeLorenzo?"

"In those ten years that he was there, there was one business transaction that I believe he, Mr. DeLorenzo, was responsible for. All the rest were my husband's."

"Does that mean that your husband kept most of the money and Mr. DeLorenzo got the credit for one transaction?"

"No," Joyce replied angrily. "It was divided fifty-fifty. I never agreed with it. I didn't think it was right and I didn't think it was fair. But that was the way it was done."

"To your knowledge," Craig asked, "did Mr. DeLorenzo have any business or conduct any sales in Bermuda?"

Joyce's voice was strong and clear now. "To my knowledge, Mr. DeLorenzo never went to Bermuda. Certainly not on company business. The only time we received, on the answering machine, phone calls that were supposedly from Bermuda was during the time that Michael was using my husband's credit card for illegal purchases in Hillsdale. I don't see how he could be in Bermuda and doing the other thing. During that time that Mr. DeLorenzo could not be found, he would occasionally call and leave a message on the office answering machine. He said he was in Bermuda on business. He was with some guy and . . . the whole thing was so bizarre, so weird. I wasn't believing any of it. My husband was coming home and telling me these things and he really wanted to believe it.

"But at that time when he was feeling so awful about the whole thing, I said, 'I could sit over here and have you come home and tell me these things and I'd think to myself that it doesn't make sense. But you were with this man all day. He was going to you all day long.'" She sighed deeply and then went on, "I can understand I guess."

Craig nodded. "You mentioned the credit cards. What was that?"

"My husband had two credit cards, Visa and MasterCharge. We decided to use the MasterCharge for business. There were people, Mr. Green and Mr. Smith who were coming to town for business and Mr. DeLorenzo didn't want my husband around. I didn't understand that. It seemed strange. But anyway, Alex gave him the credit card to take them out to dinner. When the evening was over, it was returned. It happened several times. Then, a bill came in, the card had been maxed out to five thousand dollars. Alex started talking to the MasterCharge people. There were some charges on there that Alex had not authorized. One was a cash draw for Mr. Ogdon Leeds. Alex recognized him as a friend of Mr. DeLorenzo. He called him and told Leeds to tell Mr. DeLorenzo that this was not allowed, this was not to be done and he then called MasterCharge and canceled the card. The girl talked him into having a new card issued with a different number. So he said all right. The card never came. We never received it. Michael was opening most of the mail. My husband was not at the office everyday. He was not feeling well. He was then diagnosed as having cancer.

"MasterCharge was calling about the charges on the new card but we were not getting the calls so finally the bill came in for over five thousand dollars. What had happened was that Mr. DeLorenzo had taken the card. They were all his charges. They decided to prosecute Mr. DeLorenzo for fraud, and that was done.

This was during the time when Mr. DeLorenzo was leaving messages on the phone that he was in Bermuda. It matched the date that was on the card for charges in Hillsdale."

Craig Walters kept on probing. "Was there ever any action taken by you or your husband against Mr. DeLorenzo in civil court to regain some of the losses?"

"Yes, for loans my husband had given to Mr. DeLorenzo, which he hadn't repaid, about twenty-six thousand dollars. That was all I knew about. My greatest fear was that Alex had been talked into taking out a personal loan and that I would be left with the responsibility of paying it back after Alex's death. That, however, did not happen."

Craig moved the questioning onto other matters. "Let's talk a minute about this civil action. What was involved in that?"

Joyce hesitated for a moment then said, "I have a promissory note signed by Mr. DeLorenzo for $8,000 but the total civil amount was $26,000, my husband said it was closer to $30,000 though. This was in addition to the credit card funds. I never knew everything. One of the tragic things about [the end of] Alex's cancer was that he had core-brain radiation. This made verbalization for Alex impossible. He knew things but he couldn't respond to any questions."

Craig was on a roll. "After the change over, when Mr. DeLorenzo changed the office over to another location in the building and your husband ended up paying for the phone bill, was there anymore business relationship?"

"No," Joyce replied. "Mr. DeLorenzo disappeared then. He never opened that office. He just disappeared. The last conversation my husband had with Michael, he told me about when he got home that night. He said that Michael had called. He said, 'I told him not to call me again, that we were in total adversarial positions.'"

Craig Walters continued the questioning now concentrating on the people that Joyce had met with Michael DeLorenzo socially. When he concluded, she was released from the witness stand without a single question from opposing counsel. Through it all, Michael had avoided eye contact with her, appearing for all purposes to be in a world of his own.

At day's end, testimony had been going so well that it appeared that Anna DeLorenzo's testimony would not be required at all. She had agreed to testify on Jennifer's behalf if necessary, but Craig Walters was sensitive to her discomfort. He had purposefully reserved her as a rebuttal witness to be used only if Michael began filling the record with unsubstantiated stories from the past.

As the trial drew to a close, the fascinating but not surprising fact was that the defense offered virtually no rebuttal, and no cross examination of witnesses.

Except for his testimony, only one other witness spoke for Michael's side. This witness was Alicia McNeal who he had convinced, once again, that he loved her.

At different points during the trial, Michael would make faces, laugh, and sometimes disrupt the proceedings by walking out of the courtroom in the middle of a witnesses testimony.

Finally it was his turn to testify. Michael strode to the witness box and began his repartee with his own lawyer. They went round and round during the morning session until my head ached. Finally even the judge was disgusted. The judge's indignant voice rose, "Excuse me, Mr. Hadon, your client is not even answering your questions. This is the last time I'm going to advise. After that, your client is going to be placed in a very jeopardized position. I'm going to expect over the lunch hour you tell your client to do things right." And with that he adjourned court for lunch.

◆

When Michael, having been previously sworn in, resumed the stand, his testimony continued to be hard to follow, but Mr. Hadon pursued his line of questioning. He opened by asking, "Regarding the court-ordered visitation at her maternal grandmother's, did you in any way encourage or suggest that Maria make herself unavailable for that visit?"

"I didn't." Michael's voice was a monotone. He licked his dry lips.

"There was testimony that Maria was involved in this case in that she had read an affidavit that you had prepared. Do you recall ever providing her with any affidavits in this case?"

"No I didn't." The regular volley of questions and answers was lulling and Michael's tone was flat.

"To your knowledge did she read any affidavits?" the attorney asked.

"No."

Hadon turned to another subject. He questioned Michael about Jennifer's allegations about Michael associations with the Mafia. "So you have or have you had any association with one Lennie Magalio?"

Michael nodded, "Twelve or thirteen years ago. There was a person whose nickname..."

"Was this in prison at the time you were there?" Hadon clarified.

"There was a guy by the name of Mark Robatelli, but the answer is the same," Michael explained.

"Okay. And your cell mate?"

"No. We weren't in a cell, we were in a little annex at the minimum security farm that held six people. He was my room mate."

Mr. Hadon continued, "Now, after leaving prison, did you ever have any type of communication or association with either Mr. Magalio or any of his associates?"

"No."

Hadon walked over and gave Michael a stack of papers. "Handing you what's been marked as Respondent's Number 16, and I have given counsel a copy of this, would you identify that, please?"

Looking up from the pages, Michael answered, "It's a certified copy of an order denying a rehearing in the Supreme Court of the State of Colorado."

"Well, this is a copy of all the proceedings in Colorado, is it not—Court records?" Hadon asked.

"Yes, it's a copy of all summaries of all proceedings—Court records."

Hadon identified the records further. "Okay. This is a certified copy that we asked for and you got from the State of Colorado?"

"That is correct," DeLorenzo stated.

Hadon announced decisively, turning to the judge, "I am going to offer this."

The judge looked at Walters and asked him wearily, "Do you have any objection?"

Craig Walters shook his head, "No." And the papers were admitted into evidence.

◆

A few times throughout the testimony, I was able to catch Jennifer's eye. Though she smiled weakly, I could tell she was apprehensive.

So far Michael's testimony had held no surprises. Still I couldn't help chuckling when later, Hadon asked about Michael's psychiatric evaluation.

"There was some delay in your seeing Dr. Topping. Do you know what caused that delay?"

"Yes," Michael asserted.

"What was the reason?" Hadon asked.

"I was broke," Michael said in an irritated voice.

"You had no money to pay for it?" Hadon probed.

"No."

"Was Dr. Topping willing to enter into any kind of payment program with you?"

"No." Michael fired the answers like bullets.

"Did you talk to him about a payment program?"

"I did."

"And he refused?"

"Yes."

Hadon tried to make Michael look like the victim rather than the calculating manipulator that he was. "And the only payment program that you entered into then was a court-ordered payment program?"

"Yes."

"Which he accepted?"

"Yes," Michael stated with finality.

Hadon held up his hand, "That's all I have."

◆

I was tired of Michael's lies but they weren't yet finished. Craig Walters cross examination was next. At least now the lawyer was on our side and would force Michael DeLorenzo to show his true colors.

Craig Walters began the cross examination by looking Michael straight in the eyes and asking, "Dr. Topping didn't accept a payment plan, did he? He insisted on full payment before his report was released. Isn't that correct?"

"Yes," Michael said tonelessly.

"Now, the reason that you couldn't see Dr. Topping was because you were broke and you didn't have any money to pay him and he needed money to be paid, right?" Craig slowly paced back and forth in front of the witness stand.

"Yes."

Craig gave him a confused look. "But at that time and the same period of the time you told Family Court that you were making $6,000 a month, didn't you?"

"Yes," Michael nodded definitively.

"This is the same time you were refusing requests from Jennifer and I to get access to your financial records to figure out which was really the truth, weren't you?" Craig asked accusingly.

"Yes." Michael was staring at an invisible spot on the wall.

"And during that time you had access to Gayle Higgins funds that could have been used for that purpose, didn't you?"

Michael sighed, as if bored with the questioning. "Yes. The income I had was a combination of hers and mine."

"But you could have paid one half of Dr. Topping's initial $1,500 of out of other funds if you had so chosen, couldn't you?"

Michael's voice rose in denial. "No, I couldn't."

"Didn't you have some use of the funds in Gayle Higgins' account?"

"No, I couldn't," DeLorenzo protested.

"You used those moneys for other purposes though, didn't you?"

"Needs."

"But it wasn't—needs. But it wasn't—you didn't perceive a need for Maria to get to Dr. Topping, did you?" Craig demanded.

"Of course not. Of course I did." Michael stammered, his overly confident facade beginning to crumble.

"You did. But you resisted on at least three different occasions in court," Craig pointed out.

Michael paused a moment and answered, "No."

Craig Walters continued relentlessly, "You filed affidavits saying that you didn't think she should go to Dr. Topping, didn't you?"

"I may have," Michael stated evasively.

Craig gave a half smile. "You don't remember?"

"Remember what I said in those declarations?" asked Michael, still looking a little flustered.

"You don't remember whether you told the court that you didn't think she should go to Dr. Topping?" Craig was speaking with exaggerated patience, as if to a child.

"I don't remember them. I don't know which ones you are talking about," Michael was stalling for time to collect his thoughts in preparation for the next question.

"Any of them," Craig offered.

Michael took a deep breath. "It seemed to me that he was biased, that he would be biased. He was chosen by you."

"He was chosen by the court," Craig corrected.

"No, he was chosen by—recommended by you. I recall now," Michael said, regaining his bearings. "I was waiting for an alternative to—that Gayle was working on for me through her connection in the federal court."

"The court order said Dr. Topping will be appointed unless someone else is agreed to. Isn't that right?"

"Yes," Michael nodded in agreement.

"And no one else was ever proposed. Isn't that right?" Walters looked at Michael with eyebrows raised.

"That is right."

"Now, are you telling this court now that at all times during this proceeding when what the court ordered came down saying that Dr. Topping should do an evaluation that you thought that it was a good idea?" Craig asked incredulously.

"No."

"And, in fact, you opposed it, resisted it, didn't you?" Craig insisted.

"Yes."

"And even though funds were available to do things that you thought were important, you didn't want to use those funds for Dr. Topping, did you?"

Slowly, Michael said, "I can't agree with those words the way you phrased that."

Craig ignored his answer and moved on. "Now, let's talk about attempts to get information about your financial resources. You resisted those discovery attempts as well, did you not?"

"I have no financial resources. Gayle resisted them," Michael said.

"Who represented Gayle in that resistance?"

"Who represented her? Are you talking about counsel? Or are you talking about..."

"Both," Craig interrupted.

"I was represented at the time by Byron Hadon."

"But you said Gayle was the one doing the resisting?"

"Of course."

The questions and answers were becoming harder and harder to follow. But I sat on the edge of my seat, waiting for Michael's next fabrication.

"Who was—did she represent herself in that?" Craig asked.

"Oh, excuse me. Are you talking about declarations that I filed with the information she would approve submitting to you?" Michael seemed confused.

"I am talking about going to the court and asking the court not to let us have the financial records that we were seeking." Craig's enduring patience seemed to be running out.

"When the nature of the request was so structured that counsel and Gayle and I agreed that it was not appropriate."

"But then the court ordered that you do it, didn't the court?"

"And then we did it," Michael affirmed.

Walters turned his back on Michael to look at the audience in the courtroom. "Without any fuss; is that your testimony?"

"It's not my testimony because I don't have a precise recollection of the sequence of events."

Craig went on to refresh Michael's memory. "In the sequence of events, the court had to order several times that those records be produced before they got produced."

Michael sneered. "After you went in and wanted them your way and Gayle resisted and resisted, yes, eventually you got them your way."

"Except that one portion of the request related to your tax returns, didn't it?"

"I believe so."

Craig was able to lead Michael exactly where he wanted him. "And you had control over those, didn't you, not Gayle?"

"Yes," DeLorenzo conceded.

"And you didn't produce those did you? We had to get a court order, and you had to sign in the presence of the court commissioner a request to the IRS to produce tax returns, didn't you?"

"Right, I did," Michael answered, glaring at the attorney.

"To have those sent directly to my office?"

Again Michael needed clarification, "The first set?"

"Yes."

"I don't recall what you got."

Craig Walters was holding what looked like a letter. "In fact, what I got back was a letter saying we have received..."

Hadon held up his hand, "Your Honor, objection."

Walters, angry by now, couldn't stop. "I'm asking the question."

Hadon smiled, "Counsel's testifying."

The judge sighed, "Finish your question, I'll overrule the objection. He is asking a question about a letter he got back."

◆

The testimony continued with one evasive answer after another. Questions asked, replies almost meaningless.

Suddenly, Walters turned to the subject of Michael's many marriages. "Do you recall that in answers to interrogatories you wrote down and signed a statement saying that you had married Gayle Higgins?"

"I recall that."

"In February of 1988?" Craig asked.

"I believe that to be correct."

"And then you said that you had remarried in another ceremony in April—or, excuse me—in June of 1988?"

"I did." Michael answered the routine questions calmly.

"And that ceremony took place in Bermuda?"

"It did." Michael nodded.

Craig paused and repeated, "Are you still adhering to a ceremony in Bermuda with her?"

Michael looked down at his hands, realized they were clenched into fists, and consciously relaxed them. Then, he responded to the question. "No. I lied."

There was laughter in the courtroom and some of it was mine.

On redirect Hadon asked DeLorenzo a few more questions about his Mafia ex-cellmate. When he was finished, Walters promised to be brief on his re-cross examination. He brought up the subject of Michael's income.

"Part of the information Family Court asked for was your monthly income, wasn't it?" Craig inquired.

"I presume that, yes," Michael answered.

"And that's where you said six thousand dollars a month, isn't it?"

"Yes."

"And that wasn't Gayle Higgins' income, was it?"

Michael crossed his legs as he answered, "It was not specifically delineated as such. However, I could justify it on that basis."

For a moment, Craig stopped his continuous pacing which had become consistent with the rhythm of question and answer, and looked directly at DeLorenzo, "Well, she wasn't working was she?"

"No, but she had investments."

Turning to the judge, Walters said, "I have nothing further Your Honor."

The judge rubbed his face with both hands, and breathing a deep sigh tiredly, looked at Michael. "Mr. DeLorenzo, I have a couple of questions please, I'm a little confused.

"I went back to your initial testimony that you had the other day, and at that time you testified very specifically on your examination at that time that your various living arrangements with various ladies, that your daughter, Maria called the lady—referred to her as mother; is that correct?"

"Yes."

"You also then said that she then called Gayle Higgins—is it Higgins?"

"Yes."

"—mother?" The judge did look confused.

"Yes," Michael said.

The judge coughed and took a sip of water. Then he said, "And you testified that these seemed to be kind of somewhat spontaneous, these were things she wanted to do; is that right?"

"Yes."

The judge continued. "And it was my understanding that, from your testimony, then that she had a really good relationship, particularly with Ms. McNeal, and she had a good relationship, at least for sometime, with Gayle Higgins?"

Poker faced, Michael said, "Yes."

"Okay. I have nothing else. Thank you very much." He looked at Hadon and Walters for a long moment. "Any questions gentlemen?"

The two lawyers had none and though we all were in a state of confusion due to Michael's testimony, the witness stepped down.

♦

As I had anticipated, the entire responsibility had been laid upon Maria's shoulders. Time and again when she was supposed to see Jennifer she had been told, "just refuse to go." My feeling was that if she was to be given that much responsibility by the court, Maria should also have all the facts to weigh. In that respect, Michael had all the cards.

In my opinion, when Michael testified, it was a compendium of all the lies he had spread before. It had become a litany that he recited with all the fervor of a zealot, words from a leprous mind.

Once again the specter of Ogdon Leeds was raised, the perfect marriage of many years paraded, children lauded as testimonials to his unequaled parenting, and Jennifer was blamed for the ills that had befallen him. In a deposition three years ago, Michael quoted Arthur Miller, "We are unwilling or unable to discover in ourselves the seeds of our own destruction." My vision of Michael is that long ago he plucked out his own eyes that he might never see truth revealed, and it has ever after been concealed from him.

Maria's testimony was given in camera in the judge's chambers. Only four people were in attendance; the judge, both attorneys and the court reporter. The rest of us could only speculate on what she said.

Jennifer prayed for a miracle. I prayed that, even if the outcome wasn't what Jennifer so badly wanted—custody of Maria, the child would have the opportunity to finish growing up away from the lies and deceit our ex-husband fed her as a daily diet.

Chapter Twenty-Three
Something of a Victory,
Something of a Defeat

*I*t was 10:40 A.M., and after four years of proceedings, Judge Herman Strauss, a tall graying granite featured man, arrived in court to give his summation and preliminary decision for the custody case between Jennifer Surel DeLorenzo and Michael DeLorenzo.

Judge Strauss apologized to those present for the late start explaining, "I usually can give findings; however, this is a most difficult case to give the normal findings to, since the findings in this case would only take five minutes, but the background might take an hour." Thus, in a deep sonorous voice, he began a review of the court case as he had heard it presented.

"One, the parties were divorced, and as part of a decree of dissolution that was entered at that time the father was given custody of the daughter, Maria. This appears to be a default situation that occurred when the daughter was approximately five years of age.

"Two, at the time that this occurred the mother and daughter were living in Denver and the father was living in the state of Oregon.

"Three, during a period of time, from the entry of the decree, the mother lived in Denver, Colorado and other than returning to Oregon for visits, did not change her residence until some time later . . . which was when she returned and attempted to contact and establish some relationship with the daughter and during this period found out that Mr. DeLorenzo was, in fact, in jail. The modification action was then filed.

"Four, and I don't have this in front of me, counsel, so if there is an error in what I'm saying, call it to my attention and I'll make the changes, now—a temporary order was entered which did not, in effect, change custody to the mother but did allow a third person to have the child, I believe it was Gayle Higgins at the time, and allowed a visitation arrangement to be scheduled between the mother and daughter and for the mother to pay support. A total amount of $200 per month was to be paid; $150 to the current support and $50 per month on the alleged arrearage. Evidence seems to indicate that during a period of time prior to the commencement of the modification action the father and daughter were on public assistance and the state of Oregon asserted a claim, and as a result of that claim $50 per month was being paid to the State of Oregon pending further action or ruling by the court. Evidence indicates that the mother is current in these obligations.

"Five, evidence indicates that visitation commenced between the mother and the daughter and that the visitation as scheduled seemed to be going along well, although the daughter did request for a lessening of it, which was agreed to by the mother; that during a period of time, particularly within the time frame of the proximity of the requirements of the psychological evaluations to be done by Doctor Topping, the daughter terminated visitation. I believe, until the present time, there has been no visitation and there has only been a couple of contacts with the daughter, one of which I believe was in a restaurant and the other was by telephone. There have been no visitations or contact since that time."

His voice droned on indicating his belief, so far, in what Jennifer had told him. I breathed a sigh of relief.

"Six, contrary to actions and statements of Mr. DeLorenzo, the records of the schools indicate that during the grade schooling of the child she seemed to be a fairly good student, but since her entry into the middle school and the present school her overall grades, attendance and frankly, it looks like general attitude, has sufficiently changed such that the Court would not classify her as even a fair to good student. In fact, in many of her lessons it appears that she's in very low to failing grades.

"Evidence, I believe, further shows that the father brought her to court on numerous occasions for hearings and for the first sessions waiting for trial, which I find to be extremely inappropriate, and feel simply put additional stress on the daughter, which I think is directly attributable to the conduct and to the blame of the father.

"Eight, the evidence fairly shows that just prior to the trial the daughter called the mother, and I believe the Court can classify it as a threat, stating that if the mother did not drop the action she would not see her again. The evidence does indicate that the attorney for the father did request the daughter call. However, there is no evidence that would indicate that the attorney knew that the daughter was going to make the statements that she made or that he had any part in this kind of proposed activity which the daughter relayed to the mother.

"Nine, the Court finds that based upon the facts of this case, as they have been presented, that there is a need to modify the decree of dissolution as to custody as to visitation, and as to support.

"Eleven, the evidence clearly shows that the child, Maria, has moved from place to place, in the last nine years, eleven different times. It further shows that she has been torn from relationship to relationship with different women, and that the father who had the relationship with these women, in fact, directly involved his daughter as a knowing and willing accomplice on at least one or two occasions when he committed bigamous relationships. Independent evidence indicates that, in fact, the daughter knew of this and went along with it because it was her father that did it.

"Evidence further shows that she, in fact, acknowledged this to third parties by direct testimony that was given and she admitted her part in this to other parties.

"The evidence further shows that the mother has asserted that the reason she did not carry forth with any attempt to reestablish a relationship with the daughter was as a result of the fear of violence or harm to herself and her other child. There is no question in this Court's mind, and the evidence clearly and convincingly establishes, that there were prior episodes of violence which would give rise to such a fear. Evidence further establishes that Mr. DeLorenzo made considerable threats and intimidations and frankly, got considerable mileage out of his establishing a relationship with a then known syndicate criminal, Mr. Lennie Magalio, also know as Mark Robatelli, and even kept in contact with him subsequent to his release from prison. Mr. DeLorenzo took the stand and indicated he never had contact with Mr. Magalio and, yet, evidence was established by a letter that subsequent to that time he was even writing to Mr. Magalio. This clearly goes to the impeachment of the credibility of Mr. DeLorenzo as any kind of a witness in this case.

"The Court finds that there is little question in its mind that Mr. DeLorenzo intimidated, threatened, and in the past attempted acts of violence against the mother to such a degree that she did have reason to fear for her life and did not make contact. It was interesting to note that this was further evidenced by a letter which confirms the fact that the father would not allow visitation, confirms the fact that he set terms and conditions for anything to be done, and further allows for his direct intention to disallow any contact between the daughter and the mother.

"Thus, the Court concludes that the mother Jennifer DeLorenzo had just cause to believe that Mr. DeLorenzo would carry through on his threats to harm her or her family.

"Comparing the evidence of the various witnesses, as to the credibility of these parents and their testimony, I would make certain findings within the framework of this, just as a bases for that by decision would be. Generally I have found that the bulk of the testimony of the mother has been fairly well corroborated or substantiated by third-party witnesses and I find and conclude in general she is a credible witness.

"As to the father, Mr. DeLorenzo, I find the following: He has been convicted of tax evasion. He has been convicted on three different felony crimes within the past four years. He has committed two acts of bigamy, and he has even had his own daughter intentionally involved within one of the acts of bigamy, knowing that her father was married and going along with it.

"Additionally, independent testimony shows that he deliberately misled at least two women by stating falsehoods to them as to his marital status, and by their testimony, committed bigamy, knowing at all times he was married to a third party.

"The testimony of the women, Gayle Higgins and Sofia Rinehold, both indicate that prior to their relationship with Mr. DeLorenzo they both had good jobs, were basically free of debt, basically had homes and money in the bank. Each of them showed that when Mr. DeLorenzo got through with them, both were extremely in debt, one almost lost her home, and neither party had any funds left in their accounts.

"There has also been testimony given in this trial that Mr. DeLorenzo forged the name of one of the women on credit card application which allowed him to use that for his own purposes. The Court does not understand why he should not have been prosecuted for this, but he has not been prosecuted to date.

"Evidence further shows that Alicia McNeal, who he was married to for approximately seven years, during that period of time obtained a domestic violence order and had it renewed asserting her fear of him, which simply does nothing more than substantiate the allegations of the mother Jennifer DeLorenzo that Mr. DeLorenzo is a person not to be trusted and a person whose credibility is in great doubt.

"The evidence of the various witnesses indicates that Mr. DeLorenzo, on numerous occasions, told third parties, his daughter being present on at least one of the occasions, that her mother Jennifer Surel was a thief, a liar, and mentally deranged.

"He even stated to other parties that the daughter was the product of a 'one-night stand,' as he put it, or a brief fling with a woman. All of this is shown to be false testimony. All of which he did to purposefully mislead the women and, frankly, to so alienate the daughter to her mother as to destroy any relationship.

"It should be noted at this time that the Court took considerable effort to read the report of Dr. Topping. It appears Mr. DeLorenzo didn't even have the courtesy of telling the truth. He never mentioned his felon convictions. He never mentioned the bigamous relationships. He never mentioned the fact that he had an ongoing relationship with the mother of Maria for five years. All he said was it was a short fling with a woman who destroyed his family. He never made any mention of the fact that at the time of his conduct or contact with Jennifer Surel that he was going through a divorce, but led Dr. Topping to believe that she was the beginning of what then was the divorce.

"All of this goes directly to what Dr. Topping states and, frankly, with the information given this Court gives little or no credibility to that report, unless it is otherwise corroborated or substantiated by what the report of Dr. Topping shows, which has been entered in evidence and stipulated to by counsel. This is an evaluation of Mr. DeLorenzo, Ms. DeLorenzo and the daughter Maria. I think it is most important that it be looked at because Dr. Topping was a court-appointed psychiatrist who did this evaluation. Dr. Topping is a psychiatrist who has been used by the Berk County Superior Court, as far as I know, in excess of twenty years as a court-appointed expert. In this particular case his evaluation and testimony, by way of the report, should be given considerable weight.

"It is further noted that Thomas Howard, who was the family court evaluator, found such serious concerns of the activity and actions of the father, particularly based upon independent evidence that was given, that he believed this evaluation was necessary and recommended it to the court.

"Dr. Topping has made recommendations. One of them is that he specifically finds that Mr. DeLorenzo has a major personality problem which has led to a succession of dysfunctional relationships and socially inappropriate actions. His behavior is an extremely poor model for any child going through the identity state of life. He further states that he believes that there should be unrestricted contact between the mother and the daughter. That if there is any active or passive-aggressive interference with the contacts, that he would recommend that sanctions be placed upon Mr. DeLorenzo in some way or another. He, himself, believes, within the framework of this, that the daughter—and thinks it is most important because there is little question in my mind—he believes that from what contact he has had, that the father has so turned the daughter against the mother that the relationship between the mother and daughter no longer exists, primarily because of the active participation of Mr. DeLorenzo.

"The testimony further shows, and I'm satisfied concerning this, that his conduct is such as to be totally reprehensible.

"Dr. Topping's report is accepted in full by the Court and should be made a part of the record, showing the real problems that exist in this case.

"Now, these are some of the findings that we have, and my court order will follow, then I will explain why the order is being done as such.

"I am satisfied that this father, through the testimony given by all of the third persons, including the testimony that I have reviewed and established the credibility of Joyce Solimine, the widow of Alex Solimine, Sofia Rinehold, Gayle Higgins and the report of Dr. Topping, and the report of Mr. Thomas Howard and even the testimony of Alicia McNeal—I was disturbed to some degree concerning the acts and conduct of Ms. McNeal, who has made assertions in the past of violence and yet wishes to protect Mr. DeLorenzo for what reason I cannot understand, particularly in light of the fact that he conducted himself with her as he did with most of the other women in his life, that is, using them until he is financially finished with them and then turning elsewhere.

"The testimony was very deficient. During the course of this entire trial, during the course of the material that was submitted, it became evident that Mr. DeLorenzo was evasive, did not wish to answer questions, and in fact was not truthful on numerous occasions. Based upon this, unless what was specifically said was corroborated substantially by third parties, his testimony is given with little or no weight.

"I believe that the child should be removed from the father..." Judge Strauss paused, cleared his throat and looked at Jennifer sadly.

My prayers were answered, Maria would have her chance to grow up without Michael's poisons infecting her every thought and deed.

"I find that after the Court had an in-camera proceeding with the daughter, it is not appropriate to place the daughter with the mother because I do not believe the daughter will stay. This man has so terribly brainwashed this girl that this young woman does not even understand the difference between truth and fiction. There is no question in my mind that if this Court attempts to force anything between the mother and daughter she will probably run away."

Jennifer's hopes for custody were crushed.

"Thus, it is my conclusion and it is my order that the daughter be placed in the care of a third party.

"Counsel, have either of you come up with a mutual agreement? Walters?"

Craig Walters was stoic. "There is no mutual agreement. The only comment I can make on that at this point, Your Honor, is that you indicated the time we were last in court that you were thinking about Alicia McNeal; however, your comments and findings today leave me to believe you are not as sure about her."

Judge Strauss replied, "Mr. Walters there is no question in my mind that Ms. McNeal and the daughter have a very close bond, one with the other, they truly do."

Walters was unable to remain completely calm: "I have concerns about Ms. McNeal as to the appropriateness of placement with her."

He took a deep breath and tried to keep his own emotions in check. "The only other person that we can propose would be Gayle Higgins. I have talked with her. The only way that she would consider this would be if it were clear that it was only Maria that she was taking care of, and that there would not be involvement with Michael. That's consistent with her testimony on the stand."

Judge Strauss nodded, "I understand that. Whoever the third party is, there will be a lot of restrictions put on that.

"Mr. Hadon, I asked both of you to make that recommendation. Let's hear from you as to your standpoint."

Hadon stood up giving those in the courtroom a sweeping look. "I talked to Alicia McNeal about this. She is reluctant but willing. Reluctant because you have to understand that she went through six or seven months with my client. Obviously the relationship between her and this woman are not ever going to be a close relationship. In other words, we still are looking at the same problem, regardless of where the girl lives, that is, whether or not she will willingly live there. I haven't discussed that with her, because it is not appropriate at this point."

Strauss broke in, "The Court has."

"Have you discussed this with the girl?" Hadon asked surprised.

The judge nodded. "Yes, I discussed various places and various options with the daughter in-camera, and that's all I will tell either of you at this point."

Hadon had a further point to make, "In other words, as far as I'm concerned, the problem of visitation still is one the mother has to work out."

There was a buzz of whispers from the spectators. The Judge held up his hand to get complete quiet in the court room. "We're not there yet, counsel, thank you."

Walters had both question and comment, "Your Honor?"

"Mr. Walters."

Walters went on, "Your Honor, I have a number of concerns regarding the appropriateness of placing the child with Alicia McNeal. Is this the appropriate time to express those?"

"I think so," said the judge looking Walters directly in the eyes.

Walters glared back, "One is the concern that you expressed earlier here, that given the experience that she had with Mr. DeLorenzo, some of which she didn't want to really admit to on the stand but had to because it was a matter of record, the filing of the reports, the protection order, then the renewing of that, and some of the other experiences that she had, she continues to be supportive of him. I would point out that with the exception of Mr. DeLorenzo she was the only witness that they called. She was the only person that came in and tried to explain to the Court that he was okay."

Judge Strauss shook his head. "I understand that."

"I have further concerns. As counsel has indicated...," Walters announced.

"Go ahead," Judge Strauss indicated.

"There are problems between the mother and Alicia McNeal," Walters said thoughtfully. "I think a lot of that comes from the fact, as the Court pointed out with regard to the daughter, Alicia McNeal's source of information about Jennifer Surel has been Michael DeLorenzo. So she has been exposed to, and over a long period of time, was told these same things about Jennifer that Maria was. If there is going to be any kind of—That causes two problems, one is a problem of cooperation with the mother vis-à-vis whatever kind of contact the mother and daughter will have. The other is the ongoing possibility that the child continues in this brainwashing, instead of being through Michael DeLorenzo, then through Alicia McNeal because she has the same feelings about Jennifer and they came from the same place."

Judge Strauss' long tapered fingers stroked his chin as if he was meditating for a few minutes, the room was silent. Then he said, "I just expressed this to both sides because the Court has talked with the daughter, and I had the clerk, the bailiff, and the court reporter in-camera with the daughter. She understands that her statements would not be made in court. Although there are preferences, I have a concern that whatever I do, if the daughter doesn't like it, we might have a runaway on our hands. That is a concern that is legitimate to the Court."

After the evidence presented by the plaintiff and his professed belief in it, his decision shocked the onlookers. However, he seemed to have made up his mind. "I'm going to do this: I am going to place the daughter with Alicia McNeal for a period of ninety days. I'm going to call this a cooling-off period. During that period of time the father shall have no contact with the daughter, except in the presence of Alicia McNeal, either in person or by phone. Ms. McNeal will be explicitly instructed she is to have no conversations with Mr. DeLorenzo relating to this case or anything else. If, in fact, this occurs there will be no further visitations allowed to Mr. DeLorenzo.

"At the end of the ninety-day period I will review this. If I find that Ms. McNeal has done anything intentionally to interfere with any relationship that is to be established between the daughter and the mother, the daughter shall be taken out of that residential arrangement. Ms. McNeal will be informed of this and shall follow this, if she consents to do this, that she will be required to discuss the daughter's conduct and her progress with the mother not less than two times each month by phone. The mother and the daughter, should the daughter desire, have free access to each other both by phone and by visitation.

"I am not sure that Ms. McNeal is the right person, but I know at this point that if I pick someone other than that, the daughter will rebel to the degree that I believe more harm than good will be caused.

"The Court must be completely frank and advise all parties concerned that there is no question that Ms. McNeal is one of the few people this daughter has a bonded relationship to.

"In line with this, I find that the father's conduct is such, and the daughter's conduct is such, that there is not a father-daughter relationship. There is almost an obsession. The conduct and actions of this man cause this Court extreme concern.

"I could not believe the conduct of Mr. DeLorenzo, during the course of the trial, when he would make faces and guffaw, snicker or sneer, or throw up his hands and walk out of the courtroom on occasions. This was totally inappropriate conduct at this trial or any other trial. This only gives credence to the fact that this is a man who really cannot be, and should never have been, trusted with anyone. A man who, history has shown to be one that is less than honest, less than truthful, and, frankly, less than honorable. In all the years that I have had cases I cannot believe, after what I have heard, that one would do what he did to his own daughter by so turning her against her own mother, so that she would have no relationship. It is just despicable. The record is very clear, the testimony and the evidence are very clear concerning his conduct."

The judge was grim faced. His voice steel edged. "I have gone through all the testimony and I have summarized all the testimony so that I could appropriately view this to determine what kind of conduct this man exhibited to cause his daughter to be so difficult. There is no question in my mind that he has deliberately and intentionally made his daughter into what she is.

"At the end of the ninety-day period this arrangement shall be reviewed by the court. If I find in any way that Ms. McNeal has created any problems with the mother and the daughter, or has not complied with my explicit instructions that there is to be no contact between the father and daughter other than a supervised contact with her present and there is to be no discussion about this case with the daughter, if I find this had been in any way violated the child shall be immediately removed from Alicia McNeal and a third party will then have to be found.

"I have to be frank, counsel, to let you know that I'm not satisfied that if Gayle Higgins is chosen that the daughter would stay with her. At age sixteen, I don't think we want a runaway. This is not because Ms. Higgins is a bad lady, nor are any of them bad ladies, but because the father has turned this girl against them so badly she will not stay. He has turned the daughter against them as much as he has turned the daughter against the natural mother.

"As far as support is concerned, I find that the case law is very clear that the support obligation entered was not support in direct relationship to the obligation of support to be utilized one with the other. And, in fact, the letter specifically says, just as stated from Mr. DeLorenzo to Ms. DeLorenzo, 'Just so you know I am serious, remember I could force you to pay child support, but as I told you in Colorado I have no intention to, as the amount was just punitive and I don't need it nor does my family.' Which indicates to me the point that he had no intention of enforcing the support order and used it only as a punitive wedge to keep the mother and daughter apart.

"By way of comment at this time, it is interesting to note that Alicia McNeal indicated that this conversation never took place in Colorado and, yet, he specifically refers to it happening there, which is another question that I have with Alicia McNeal," Strauss said uncertainly but then he went on, his voice hardening. "So, I think, Mr. Hadon, you will have to explain to Ms. McNeal the rules of the game. If you don't, the child will not be there. I want you to understand that.

"Now, as to the area of estoppel and latches, I cite you the case of In Re Goldberg vs. Jones, particularly that, in this case, there was no intention to enforce the support. Please look at Consuelo vs. Mira, 100 Oregon 2d 766, and 42 Oregon App 371, which is In Re The Marriage of Tate. In both instances the conduct of the recipient parent was such as to make the other parent believe that support would not have to be paid; or if it is not now being enforced, it is so inappropriate as not to allow it to be done.

"I find, as the court did in Goldberg vs. Jones, that the mother specifically relied on the father's recitations that support was not to be used as support but only as a punitive wedge to stop visitation, so that any attempt to enforce support prior to the commencement of the modification action is disallowed. Any money paid to the State of Oregon on support arrearage shall be consider to be payment of support in the future to third parties until it is completely taken care of. I think it was $50 a month for some fifteen or twenty months, something like that, plus other moneys."

The judge continued in a similar vein for a time on how support for Maria would be paid and by which part, health insurance and counseling. A counselor, Loren April, was named as well as attorney's fees awarded, citing the additional expense created by Mr. DeLorenzo in his delaying tactics. Then he returned to the critical question of Maria's placement.

"Have I covered everything in this matter counsel?" the judge asked.

Hadon shook his head, "Not quite to my satisfaction. Alicia McNeal lives in the Silverrock area. The girl is in school at Hayes High School. School isn't out over there until June 22nd. Somehow it seems to me it is inappropriate at this point to require her to leave Hayes High School and go to some school out in the Silverrock area. For obvious reasons, I don't see any solution to it."

"Where does Gayle Higgins live?" the judge asked.

Craig piped up, "She lives in the district where Maria is going to school. That's where Maria started going to school, when she started living with her."

Judge Strauss looked tired and exasperated by this time. "At this point, I will reconsider my placement with Alicia McNeal," he paused and gazed at Michael DeLorenzo pensively, "and place the child with Gayle Higgins until school is out. At that time, I will review it. I don't want to disturb the daughter anymore than necessary."

"All with the same limitation?" Walters queried.

"I don't care who the girl is with, those limitations will be there in the future," Judge Strauss snapped.

The judge rubbed his forehead with his fingers, "There is no question in my mind that Mr. DeLorenzo has done a number on his own daughter. This is the most disturbing and distressing thing I've had to deal with in the thirty years of my doing this crazy business, no question about it."

As the last details were covered, the judge returned once more to his observations of Maria DeLorenzo.

"The Court will make, on the record, the following observations of the daughter: This daughter does not even understand, at times, right from wrong. She doesn't even understand, at times, truth from fiction. There is no question in my mind it is because of what she was taught by the father. If it were not that this is so serious, this so reminds me of the movie with Ryan and Tatum O'Neal called *Paper Moon*, where the father took the daughter and made her his own shill. It is unfortunate, but it happened." He shook his head angrily.

Then he instructed Byron Hadon to tell Maria of the Court decision regarding her and complete the transfer in three days time.

◆

Later that afternoon, Jennifer reached her car in time to see Michael and Maria leave the parking lot with the woman we knew as Cindy Emery. Jennifer's initial reaction was a stab of fear that Michael might flee. Then she thought he might have done something to her car, then a third more composed thought, why is the woman still with them?

He had ordered the transfer of custody to take place the following Monday; however, on that day, Hadon and Michael DeLorenzo returned to court only to tell the judge that Maria refused to go. The judge demanded that they bring her to court on the following Friday.

On Friday no one appeared.

When Michael failed to show up for the Friday hearing I began to worry that he had used his new girlfriend's money to skip town with Maria. This translated into fitful sleep. I could not stop thinking of Cindy Emery and wondered whether she had been warned by anyone of Michael's background and his forgeries. After several sleepless nights I decided I had to warn her myself.

Since she was probably with Michael I looked in the telephone directory for the number of Cindy's ex-husband Todd Emery. I picked up the receiver and dialed. A male voice answered the ring almost immediately.

"Is this Todd Emery?" I inquired.

"Yes, it is," he replied.

"Has either the Hillsdale Police Department or an attorney's office contacted you regarding the man your ex-wife is currently living with?" I asked, my lower lip quivered.

"No," he answered slowly.

I gathered my courage. "Let me take a moment to explain who I am, and why I am calling. Do you have a little time?" I asked feeling my way along.

"Yes. Please go on," he replied quietly.

"My name is Sofia. We are neighbors. I have some court documents that I'd like to share with you concerning this man. It might be a little easier to let you read them than try to explain them over the telephone. Would you mind if I drop by?"

"No. That sounds like a good idea. My house is a little messy because my college-age son lives with me, but..."

"I'm not coming on a house tour I promise," I broke in, laughing in some relief. "I just live a short distance away so I'll probably just walk over. I'll see you in a few minutes."

That was the beginning of an extraordinary evening. As Todd read the judge's findings and learned of Michael DeLorenzo's criminal background, forgeries, bigamy and con activities his incredulity changed to amazement and then to deep concern for his ex-wife Cindy's physical and financial well-being. We discussed how she might be reached without Michael learning of it, and how the material could be presented so she would look at it without Michael being able to influence her into rejecting it before she had a chance to assimilate the information and make some objective judgments.

I suggested the best method might be to have their son call Cindy and ask her to come over, pretending he had a personal problem. That way it would be less likely that she would bring Maria, or alert Michael that trouble was afoot for him. I left Todd with a photocopy of Judge Strauss' findings. I said goodnight. I felt pleased with myself but tense as I returned home. To my surprise that night I slept like a baby.

It was two days before Todd called me back. "Tonight is our meeting with Cindy."

When Cindy arrived, their son, Jason, met her outside. He told her that he had copies of the judge's summation and if she wanted to read them she'd have to come inside. As she came through the front door I heard her say to him, loudly, 'I know all this.'

"You think you know," I interjected. "Well, Cindy, you don't know all of it."

We sat her down and showed her the briefs. She went through a lot of different emotions. She was reading, crying, going back and forth reading and reading the accusations about Michael. At each point of accusation she defended him. "I'm aware of the prison stint and about the income tax evasion," she said nervously as she read on.

"What about bank fraud and theft of corporate funds," I offered.

She shook her head. "No," she said, her calm breaking.

"The court record made mention of three felony convictions but I wasn't sure if he was serving concurrently for that or not, Sofia," Todd interjected.

"It was since that time," I added. "Those were three felony convictions in the last four years the judge was referring to, as well as credit card theft and forgery. This is ten years after his first prison stay, for the IRS conviction," I clarified.

Cindy said, "I am aware of Jennifer and Gayle, and you too." She pointed to me. Todd kept mispronouncing my name and she kept correcting him. Then she paused.

I wanted to add a little levity to the tense atmosphere, "Gayle Higgins believed that I was the housekeeper," I said laughing. "That's how Michael explained me to her. Heaven only knows what you've been told. It changes from year to year and occasion to occasion, who or what I might be. It is amazing. What is really sad is that Maria is all woven into that."

"Everyone likes Maria," Todd said. "I like Maria, the kids like Maria. . ."

"Of course they do, she's darling. She's also part and parcel of what goes on. Michael would not be able to swindle these women for long if Maria didn't back his lies."

"Dr. Topping's report says Michael has so brainwashed this girl she doesn't even know right from wrong anymore, and as long as it's her father that's doing it, well it's got to be okay. You know and I know that you must take responsibility for your actions. Michael has destroyed Maria's moral values," I declared with feeling.

"Is she going to have counseling?" Todd asked quietly.

"I hope so. It's in the court orders. They have even named a counselor. It's one of the things that Jennifer fought so hard for, to get her daughter into counseling to try to undo some of the tremendous damage Michael has done to Maria. Michael fought tooth and nail to avoid the psychological evaluation by Dr. Topping. In my opinion, Michael knows he is not normal and he was afraid it would show up and it did. Topping said Michael has a major personality disorder."

"And there is nothing wrong with Jennifer?" Cindy asked.

I shook my head. "There is nothing wrong with Jennifer except she has had her daughter stolen from her and destroyed. That's what's the matter with Jennifer," I said emphatically.

"So the stories that Jennifer is unfit and a liar. . ." Cindy said shuffling through the court papers.

"Are untrue," I finished the sentence. "None of it is true, it's been disproved over and over again in court. In Colorado Jennifer worked for Child Welfare, here she is in an Office of Environmental Affairs. She's a very bright lady, very capable. Can you imagine someone with that kind of record being unfit? They run background checks on all city applicants. Believe me they'd know," I said in disgust.

As we talked I saw Cindy starting, in her mind, to question Michael. Even so there were other moments when I could see she was still going through denial.

"Are you going to talk to the police?" I asked hopefully.

"I think so," she said and then she answered, "I don't know, " she got up. "I really have to go. We're going to Bermuda tomorrow or in the next few days. She looked at me. I shook my head and stared directly into her eyes."

After she left, Todd and I talked some more as he walked me home. "If she confronts Michael and he starts his oily talk. . ." I began.

"I'll bet you anything she won't."

"That man can talk his way around anything," I offered.

"Even if she does confront him, I'm not sure it would do any good," Todd said.

"Remember how she kept flipping back and forth through the court papers. When she found the part on the bigamy she looked shocked." Todd paused. "What do you think about the Bermuda trip?"

"They were supposed to leave tomorrow, right?" I asked. He nodded. "It's always postponed. I've heard it all before. It's always something. 'Oh well, we can't go tomorrow because Jennifer had done something to Maria's passport or my business partner has this female problem and she's in the hospital.' I can guarantee you one thing, Todd. If they ever do fly to Bermuda it will be on Cindy's money, not his," I emphasized. "If not her money directly, indirectly by his forging her name on a credit card and charging it. That way he is not paying for it. That's the way he operates."

"At least she is getting into the doubting stage," Todd added.

"Yes, but there is still a lot of denial. Cindy still doesn't want to face up to the fact that she made a big mistake," I sighed. "It's very hard to do that. That's understandable when you know how good he is at manipulation," I added.

"Maybe she'll move out," Todd said hopefully.

"Maybe," I said remembering Janet Solimine's testimony. Suddenly, I had an anxious thought, "Was the apartment lease put in her name or his?"

"I'm not really sure," Todd replied. "Right now I think both of them are paying half the rent."

"You'd better find out because if she moves out, he'll stop paying the rent and she'll get stuck with it," I warned. "He is completely undependable. Last week he was supposed to come back to court to show cause why he hadn't turned Maria over to the court. He didn't even show up."

"I guess Cindy's never actually heard any of the testimony?" Todd asked.

I shook my head, "No way in hell would he let her sit in court and hear all these people testify."

"Was it a closed hearing?" Todd asked.

"Oh no, anybody could go in. Michael wouldn't have said, 'please don't go in.' What he would have said, was, 'You take Maria and keep her nearby, I don't want her to run into her mother. It might be too uncomfortable for her.' He would have this whole spiel so that she would not want to go into the courtroom," I explained.

"I told Jennifer a while ago, 'So help me, if I ever see a woman with Michael, in a cafe, on a street, anywhere at all, I'm going to go right up to them and warn her. If he has a heart attack or hits me and I end up on the floor that's too bad. I don't care, I will not be silent. There is nothing that he can do about me telling the truth about him. Nothing at all.'"

"No," Todd affirmed quietly.

"What can he say? That I lied about him?" Todd and I began laughing at the incongruous idea.

"I expect not," Todd replied, still chuckling.

Todd was silent and thoughtful for a short while, then spoke. "Michael owes Cindy money. Not much, relatively speaking. She told me a while ago she loaned him $3,600."

"It's not what you know about that concerns me," I interjected, "it's that he might have gotten credit cards in her name without her knowledge."

"She caught him trying to do just that three weeks ago. She just happened to be home when the bank called to confirm the request," Todd said disgustedly. "I asked her then, 'Why are you still with him Cindy?' and she just looked away."

We talked a while longer then Todd left and walked the short block back to his home. Amazingly, for years we had lived only eight houses apart, never knowing one another.

◆

A short while later, Cindy moved out of the apartment she shared with Michael. She left him just eight days after my first phone call to Todd. Afterward, Michael sent word to me, through Todd, that he knew what kind of car I was driving. A few days later, I left work to find the windows in my car broken again. I guess that Michael wanted to be certain that I got the message.

*N*ow that it's all over, it's pointless to wonder how or why I became involved in the DeLorenzo custody case. I think it was inevitable from the moment I found out the truth about Michael DeLorenzo because of who I am and what I feel is important. I know I won't end my involvement until I'm no longer needed.

Gayle Higgins called me last night to ask for help. Not only has Michael wiped out her savings, but he's ruined her credit. "Please," she asked, "can you help me?"

Today I went to the Second National Bank to plead Gayle's case.

Maria was never surrendered to the court for placement with Gayle. She finally appeared at Alicia's several weeks after the trial. Frustrated and angry, the judge let the placement stand. Alicia returned Maria to the court. She was tired of the games, lack of child support, and Michael's trying to circumvent the court directives. She realized she too had become the enemy. Michael tried to regain custody. Fortunately, hours before the hearing, Jennifer's attorney became aware of the court proceeding and successfully blocked it. The judge still felt Maria wouldn't stay with Jennifer; so Maria was placed in a Forster home.

After Maria's placement, she was appointed an attorney of her own and appeared in court for the first time. The court experience exposed Maria to information regarding her mother she never had access to before. She had never been told that she [herself] had to initiate contact in order for Jennifer to have visitation. Moreover, Maria had not received the counseling she needed and that the court had directed.

Maria began to attend counseling sessions. Six weeks later Jennifer was asked to attend a joint counseling session with Maria and her psychiatrist. The issue of self-esteem and the subtle and not so subtle ways Michael attacked Maria through painting Jennifer as an evil person were addressed.

After that session Jennifer was invited to have dinner with Maria and then see Maria's bedroom at the foster home.

Their relationship is very slowly growing as Maria begins to gain some insight into the ways she has been used by her father. However, it is a very slow process. Maria still is very protective of the father she loves so desperately. Nevertheless, in the not so distant future, Jennifer will no longer be vulnerable to Michael DeLorenzo's peregrinations and cyclical trips to court since Maria will be eighteen years of age.

Michael's mother died recently, at age ninety-four. His other children have little to do with him but there are those who are interested in what he does. The men in blue who watch and wait.

Michael DeLorenzo is seen occasionally in the area east of Portland. Although he was charged and convicted of other crimes. He was never prosecuted for bigamy even though I wrote, including all the evidence, to the Prosecuting Attorney's Office. There simply was no response.

I also attempted to get an investigative reporter from the Oregon Herald to look into the facts of the case. I was told, "off the record," I'd have better luck with a newspaper published outside of the Portland region.

One year later:

Cindy Emery decided to relocate where Michael DeLorenzo couldn't find her. She was leaving on Tuesday for Australia.

We all decided to meet for dinner the day following Mother's Day. It would be an exclusive club; no dues would be required since we'd all paid heavily in advance.

Cindy arrived right on time. Her long light brown hair was loose and she looked pretty though her face appeared strained. Nevertheless she smiled and said, "Hello, you don't know how glad I am to see you all, post you know who." Her engaging upbeat spirit showed through. Jennifer arrived minutes later.

"Michael was an unfortunate and expensive lesson for a lot of people," I said.

"I know," Cindy replied openly. She held nothing back, even her own pain. "I never did anything to hurt him. He has hurt so many people. I just found it so difficult to believe that anyone could be that bad. I had a lot of trouble accepting that he could be as bad as I was afraid he was. Now, there is no doubt in my mind," Cindy said. "But, he's got somebody else now, and—"

"That doesn't surprise me at all," Jennifer broke in. "I don't want you to think that I'm going to say this to hurt you, but there has always been another woman, all along."

Gayle and Alicia repeated the same thing. Gayle added, "Oh, Cindy, there is always going to be another woman. There always has been and there will always be. He told me that until he met

Jennifer, he'd been faithful to Anna. His affair with Jennifer consisted of a one night stand. When we met, he said he hadn't been with a woman since he divorced Alicia. Then, I found out he had married two."

Cindy chuckled helplessly. "My God. He said he'd been living in Bermuda trying to get over the divorce and didn't think he ever wanted to try another relationship until he met me."

"It sounded good," we echoed in unison.

"It does make you very leery about the future," Jennifer said disgustedly. "But I've met and talked to a lot of people. I know that Michael is an exception. Not everyone is like that, but I tell you, it's hard to trust again."

Cindy added slowly shaking her head, "It hurt a lot. Not only did he rob me of my feelings of self-worth, Michael owes me money. He's made me crazy with his lies. I'm convinced he doesn't know when he's lying or telling the truth."

We all chimed in, "Us too."

"If you want your money back, you'll have to make a claim for it," I counseled.

"He doesn't have a dime so. . ." Cindy paused then looked at us. "Do you think he does?" she asked quizzically.

"My personal opinion is that he borrows money from one woman to spend on another. So, these women see that he always has cash or checks. It keeps them off guard when he borrows money from them because it seems he does have some other source. I think that's how he keeps it going on," Jennifer commented.

"Besides," I interjected, "it was leaving a money trail before that the FBI could follow that sent Michael to prison. He's not likely to make the same mistake twice. When he bought my diamond ring with a bogus check, he went to prison for theft and grand larceny. Later, when he bought Gayle's ring, the money was real, and the diamonds were fake. I don't think Michael will ever be without, at least for himself. Somewhere he has the money he took illegally. It may be in an old mattress, in a storage unit, or tucked away under assumed names in a dozen banks. It's somewhere, I'm certain of it," I stated emphatically. "However, I don't believe there is a trust fund for Maria of any kind. He's too selfish for that. But, the money exists. At least a hundred thousand of Alicia's, seventy-two thousand of Gayle's, plus yours Cindy, and who really knows how much left over from the insurance money he got many years ago. It's never been recovered."

We looked at one another in silent commiseration. Then Cindy spoke. "I loaned him a credit card, so he could buy Maria a few Christmas gifts. The custody trial was going on and he said, 'Oh, if you get this Citibank credit card, I'll just pay you after this is over.' He charged up to the limit, and I'm left making payments on it. He is the most despicable snake. I can't believe that afterward, he tried to get another credit card, in my name, through Visa-Gold. They sent me an application in the mail. I threw it away. Michael fished it out of the garbage, filled it out and sent it in requesting a credit card to be sent to his private post office box. I happened to be home when they called to confirm his request and check whether I had approved it."

"You were lucky," we chorused in reply.

She nodded. "And I said, 'You son-of-a-bitch.' That did it. I had to protect all my investments after that, to the point it's even hard for *me* to get to them. But if it wasn't for that he'd have gotten a heck of a lot more." Cindy sighed disgustedly then went on. "He used to tell me, 'Just stick with me baby, you'll never be sorry.' I went back and forth. I'd get in a row with him and throw him out. Then he'd call me and call me and I'd give in. It would start all over. I really cared about him and I couldn't believe he could be that bad. Even the psychologist I was seeing was conned. Michael saw her and tried to get her to testify at the trial. He never paid her. Later, she told me, 'Cindy, I came close to making a complete ass of myself in court.' For myself, I wanted him to prove, for once and for all, that he wasn't lying. It was always 'give me until the fifteenth, another week or two.'"

Suddenly Cindy's conversation took an abrupt turn. "I'd love to know what he's doing now."

"Maybe he's dummied up a diploma of some sort," I interjected. "He's never graduated from school."

"He told me he graduated from Wharton," Cindy said in disgust.

"He didn't," I replied. "Nor was he an officer in the Navy. He never served overseas."

"Where did he get all those papers, then?" Cindy asked in amazement.

"He probably makes them himself. He's very creative." Jennifer replied.

"Or possibly alters legitimate papers picked up in a garage sale." I offered, remembering my own disgust at learning the truth.

"At the end, I called him a Con-Juan to his face." Cindy gave a bitter smile and drank a sip of water. "I wouldn't even leave my purse behind when I went to the bathroom. I told him I didn't trust him, that he hadn't proved to me that I could. He still wanted me to marry him," Cindy added. "I wouldn't. I told him, 'I won't marry you until I have met every one or your children, until you have been out of trouble for years, and have proved to me that you are not what other people say you are.'" After a few moments, which Cindy spent staring at the water glass in her hand, she said, "I'm so embarrassed I've even been seen with him. I must be stupid."

"You're not stupid. He's very good at manipulating people. He's fooled a lot of people," I replied in sympathy. "He's fooled judges, attorneys, lots of women, bankers; all intelligent people."

"You know what he told me now? Who he's living with?" Cindy asked softly. "Catherine Post Richards."

A sudden pandemonium of loud laughter erupted from all of us shattering the quiet restaurant atmosphere. "It's a ridiculous statement. We all have heard the myth before. Michael's jet-set paramour, business partner, heiress to millions. Her fame has grown since I'd heard it first as Catherine Richards, now I guess Post had been added," I sighed.

"You don't really believe she exists do you?" Jennifer blurted out.

I shook my head. "One of the things the police found in the empty apartment at the welfare housing when they arrested Michael were pages of photos and pseudo-background material on Michael's prospective heiress-wife Catherine. The DeLorenzo estate in the Somersett Area of Bermuda was actually Greely Acres owned by a friend of mine. Michael took the photos during a visit we made there the day following our marriage. The picture offered as Catherine Richards was me." I looked at Cindy who didn't seem surprised.

"I saw him last Tuesday. We met at a restaurant and what does he bring with him but a shopping bag of pictures he claims is Catherine Post Richards. He says she's buying him a townhouse in Hillsdale, a brand new Jaguar. He showed me a new picture of Catherine at her estate in Ireland. According to Michael's story she wants him to go there and write." Cindy stared at us in confusion.

"She doesn't exist," Jennifer said definitively. "Whoever the woman is in those new pictures, I hope she is more skeptical than the rest of us. There is no such person as Catherine."

"I think I've known that for a long time." Cindy bit her lip angrily.

"Cindy," I hesitated a moment searching for the right words. "There is something I've wondered about. Why did you continue to see Michael after you moved out? You were warned by so many people about him."

Cindy shook her head, "I know it doesn't make any sense. I really cared for him and I couldn't believe anyone could be as bad as what I'd been told. I didn't want to believe Michael wasn't what he told me he was. He always told me what a wonderful father he had been. The stories of successfully raising his family, the exotic trips he took them on and all the things he did for them. He made me believe he was so wonderful, and all those stories about the luxury hotels and huge malls he built and the compound in Bermuda where he lived. I didn't want to believe it wasn't true. How can you accept that everything a person has ever told you is a lie?"

I didn't reply. We all had found out the truth the hard way but to me denial was far worse than accepting the reality of Michael's true character.

"Alicia, you told me."

Alicia nodded.

"And so did my psychologist," Cindy continued. "She said that Michael is a sociopath and a pathological liar and when a person is that ill there is absolutely no help or turning back. He is a very sick man."

"You could tell that from what he has done to Maria. Nobody who wasn't unbalanced, would do that to their own child," Jennifer objected.

"What about what Michael told me about not having been with a woman since they had divorced. Why didn't Maria tell me? It hurt me so badly."

"She couldn't. Maria just couldn't. I think she is afraid of him," Jennifer reported.

"He has drummed into Maria's head that she is not to defy him, that includes not contradicting his lies. He tells her, 'If you are disloyal it means you don't love me. You owe it to me to be loyal because I've done all this suffering for you. If you defy me I'll die. I'll have a heart attack and die,'" I explained. "I know only too well how true this is. Long ago Maria had confided to me those very words. Maria could not leave Michael. Though she was only a child of twelve at the time, she felt responsible for him."

"He told me once," Cindy offered, "about a week after we had a big fight, that he had been in a hospital and it was my fault. I asked him what hospital? He told me it was Saint Francis and he had seen a Father Ferdinand there who wanted to give us counseling. I called Saint Francis's. He'd never been in there."

"Surprise, surprise!" Jennifer's winsome face scrunched up as she chirped, and we all began to laugh.

I interjected, "He's very sick and it's unfortunate because there are a lot of us who have been hurt very deeply and will have scars forever, especially the children," I commented.

"I don't know where your relationship with Maria is now," Cindy said to Jennifer. "Do you think it will ever improve?"

"Very slowly," Jennifer replied.

"It will probably not be wholly healed until Maria's an adult but at least we've opened the door," Jennifer added.

"I think Alicia is basically a very nice person. She doesn't have a very high opinion of Michael. The reason she did take Maria was to get her away from his influence." Cindy's voice dropped almost to a whisper. I leaned forward to hear her. "I just hope Maria gets her head together. She's such a sweet, beautiful girl and it so sad Michael has harmed her so much." Cindy's expression conveyed as much emotion as her impassioned words. She took a handkerchief from her pocket and dabbed at her eyes.

Wanting to change the subject, I chimed in, "Well, who gets to tell the police where he is?"

For a long moment all of us at the table looked sympathetically at each other. Each of us had good reasons to want to be the one. Cindy held up her hand. "I'll do it before my trip to Australia. It's only fitting, I'm his last victim—at least for now."

We all nodded in agreement. A few minutes later, the waitress served our coffee.

I glanced at my watch. It was late. "Before we leave, let's drink a toast to our success," I said. "We may not have achieved all we desired," I paused and glanced sadly at Jennifer, then determinedly went on, "but we've achieved the most important element. We've reclaimed our lives." I smiled again, and each of the women joined me as she lifted her coffee cup. "Michael once told Maria that marrying me was his biggest mistake. I believe I proved him right."

It's an odd feeling to sit surrounded by documents cataloguing the events of disrupted lives—five marriages, many at the same time, each ending in divorce or annulment, each to the same man. The similarities in all the documents are striking, especially the redundant protection orders and records of violence. They indicate the mental stress that we all suffered including even suicide attempts for some. It's an even odder feeling because my own annulment of a marriage that never really existed legally is amongst them.

As I began investigating the stories of the women whose lives, like mine, had been so irrevocably changed by their relationship with Michael DeLorenzo, I was quite struck by the collective vulnerability, and the similar reasons that kept us all tied to Michael DeLorenzo, in some cases through years of abuse.

Looking back at our relationships with Michael, I found that an intense period of courtship was present in every case. Michael's pursuit was always characterized by his complete and possessive bonding. If he wasn't present he would call several times a day to talk to the woman he wanted at the time. There are few things so irresistible than a man who seems completely captivated by you.

Michael seemed interested in knowing everything about the woman he was dating—what she did, how she felt about things, what she liked. He encouraged her to talk and wherever he was at the time sat there gazing directly into her eyes.

He would follow that intent listening with his own story of deprivation as a child and tremendous success as a father, as a businessman, and his devastation after losing his first wife of many years. Often this was followed by his saying he never believed he would—whichever woman he was now seeing—be interested in becoming involved again, until he met "her." Michael's courting was a fantasy of romantic love, excitement and expectations.

Michael never allowed time for the woman he was dating to think. He kept the courtship at a whirlwind pace and added many exciting dimensions to it with plans for wonderful trips, new homes and other impressive activities. He'd invent outrageous charades to flatter and impress the woman such as when he called a fashionable dress shop in Bermuda to reserve the shop exclusively for buying my trousseau. With me listening, he told the shop owner, "Set aside everything you have in a size eight. No other customers should be allowed in the shop during our appointment." Michael told me he would personally select or approve all the clothing.

The frenzy and excitement engendered was always so contagious others got caught up in "the romance". Asking her family or friends to fly expense free to exotic destinations further binds the woman to the fantasy. Emotions become so strong that they cloud perceptions. Anything that might block the created image of the perfect romance is ignored. Of course, red flags were there for each woman Michael courted to see, but we all were so focused on Michael and how he made us feel that logic was lost.

If Michael had spoken of how greedy and self-serving his first wife was and how she was only there for the good times, Jennifer, Alicia, Gayle, Cindy or I, as well might have looked closer at his opinion of women but he didn't. He visited his aged mother often in the nursing home and spoke with feigned reverence of his first wife Anna who divorced him "after many beautiful years of marriage."

By that time we were hooked; we were ready to ignore everything that did not fit into the rose colored picture we were creating. Michael's lack of dependability was written off as a temporary problem. His intensity was proof of his commitment to each relationship and we all focused on that. He spoke of "melding families together, starting anew and creating a home free of bad memories," We swallowed the bait. Our senses of self became secondary to the relationship. As time passed work was given up, friendships and other activities such as hiking and oil painting or gardening were replaced by meeting Michael's needs or demands.

Each of the women with whom he became involved, in varying degrees, also became Michael's rescuer, making her feel needed. Not only did Michael present himself as needing love and healing, there was Maria—a sweet child in desperate need of mothering.

By providing the comfort of a home and family environment we all became caught up in our hopes for his transformation. I recommended Michael to a friend, Dr. Martin Glade, for hypnotism/counseling to lower his blood pressure, and I personally manicured his bitten nails.

Dr. Susan Forward describes the difference between "helping and rescuing" in her book, *Men Who Hate Women & The Women Who Love Them*. She says that there is a large gap between helping and rescuing. "We all need help over the rough spots in life from time to time. Rescuing, on the other hand, is a repetitive behavior. The man always needs your help and is usually in difficulties."

The charismatic power of a person's darker side, exciting, brilliant and potentially deadly is strong. The moment in the relationship when Michael revealed himself was critical. He wanted to be sure of how a woman responded. This would set a pattern that would replicate itself again and again like a cancerous cell.

The pattern was present in all our relationships. Rationalizing Michael's behavior, for many years, finding or accepting excuses for his inability to keep a steady job kept Anna in bondage. She told herself his cruel and abusive behavior was temporary and only a response to his being under pressure.

Jennifer accepted Michael's outbursts with the same equanimity. She told herself they just happened because of the IRS/FBI problems and his divorce. She excused his drinking too much because of pressure. She told herself it wasn't his fault and that he can be so wonderful.

Alicia blamed Jennifer and Michael's unwarranted financial problems for his behavior. She felt her own emotional difficulties were not his fault but hers.

Gayle blamed the custody trial and its attendant problems and the stress of Michael serving jail time for his actions.

And I, I believed all he said and seemed. However, in every case, the verbal attacks and the lies increased to the point that the women began to doubt themselves. Jennifer, for instance, began keeping a journal, writing down things Michael told her and jotting dates on a calendar to reassure herself she wasn't losing her mind.

As the woman became more disillusioned and suggested Michael might need help or therapy, Michael began attacking her. She was blamed for being unstable and incapable of loving. Even his first wife whom he later praised was labeled as having "a water faucet type of love." Love that she could turn on a little bit at a time, full blast or not at all. Michael never accepted responsibility for his own behavior and the cycle would repeat itself once more.

All of the women who loved him were vulnerable. For instance, Anna was only shortly out of high school when they married. Like many of the young Catholic women of her generation she was expected to wed young and begin a family. She stayed with Michael through a long and difficult marriage, supporting the family with the help of her older children and Michael's widowed mother.

After years of sporadic employment Michael resorted to criminal activity. The divorce was precipitated by a succession of events including an F.B.I./Internal Revenue investigation and the birth of an illegitimate child fathered by Michael. Anna's decision to separate and divorce Michael came at a dear price. It nearly cost Anna her life.

Jennifer Surel was alone and unemployed when a friend told her about a job opening. Within two months of being hired as Michael's assistant she became involved in a relationship with him and shortly thereafter became pregnant. She was caught up in the turmoil of Michael's divorce and the IRS/FBI investigation. Jennifer became both his rescuer and codependent in an ever escalating abusive/addictive relationship.

Jennifer stuck with Michael for a long time believing that things would someday get better and their relationship would again be the way it was when she first met him. It wasn't until it was almost too late that she learned how cruel and vindictive Michael could be.

Alicia McNeal was introduced to Michael by a mutual friend. She had recently been widowed and though she was financially well off she was lonely and susceptible to Michael's persistent pursuit. Michael often brought his four-year old daughter Maria with him to visit Alicia and talked of divorcing Jennifer and raising Maria alone. When Jennifer left the state taking Maria with her Michael obtained a divorce and custody.

Then Michael married Alicia and enlisted her in his campaign to separate Jennifer from her daughter. Alicia was tightly bound to Michael and Maria by her feelings for Michael, the intensity of the battle over Maria and the sweetness and tender age of the child.

Michael was able to cover his inadequacies for years, according to the court testimony of Joyce Solimine, because her husband split the office receipts fifty-fifty despite the fact that Michael did not bring in business to the company. Eventually, through the loss of their home and the repossession of their boat and other possessions Alicia lost a lot of her faith in Michael. As in the two divorces preceding hers, threats, violence, mental health counseling and criminal activity crept into the paperwork. Michael was charged with forgery. Alicia applied for protection saying Michael was following her. He disappeared, but he called her often.

He was obsessed with knowing her whereabouts and drove past her home daily.

In his relationships, Michael vacillated back and forth between complete control and fear of abandonment. He followed a typical pattern of behavior for a misogynist: he would cry, beg, break down and promise to do better. As with the rest of us who he victimized, he would remind Alicia of all the good times they shared and how much he still loved and needed her.

However, if Alicia's testimony in court reflected her innermost feelings, her words that "they probably made a mistake in divorcing" bears the unmistakable mark of one still clinging to an irrational belief. Was she blaming herself for the forgery convictions he received after their separation? He may have used the same hook with Alicia that he used with Anna and then later with his daughter, Maria, making her believe that he would not survive if she left him. He'd talked of suicide for years.

In my opinion, Michael was looking for a haven, a person to rescue him. When we met, he was being sued by his former business partner for grand theft and forgery and sued for divorce by his wife. He and Maria were living in welfare housing. She spent many hours there alone while Michael pursued me. A frightening and lonely experience for a young girl.

When we met, I had recently returned from a lonely vacation in Europe my first vacation since my trying divorce. My jewelry and BMW advertised a much wealthier woman than I actually was and I became a mark. Michael devoted himself to learning as much about me as he could concentrating on my values and dreams. He learned of my devotion to my children, especially my deaf daughter and used that knowledge in his efforts to manipulate me.

It is easy to manipulate a vulnerable person for much of what we believe about another person, when we first meet them, is based on the information that they provide. If you understand their dreams and embroider yourself with their perfect design they'll see no faults. It's a perfect camouflage.

Michael presented himself as the perfect father. He made elaborate plans for our home together. He was much older than I and in many ways seemed to replace the generous and loving father I'd lost as a child. He also seemed to have the attributes missing from the husband and father that had walked out on me and my children without ever looking back.

I was fortunate that I had a more stable background than the other women Michael married. I came from a loving home and never learned codependent behavior. I was also invested with a strong moral code as a child. Illegal behavior was not condoned; rather, it was cause for being ostracized.

When Michael was arrested he found no rescuer in me. Instead I threw him out. Michael wasn't accustomed to the reaction he got. His deeds made my ears deaf to his pleading, and words were all he had.

Gayle Higgins, the woman Michael married after me was charmed by him just as I had been. When I threw Michael out he began pursuing Gayle in earnest. He needed a new place for himself and Maria to live.

Gayle was especially vulnerable to Maria. She was near the age Gayle's daughter was when she was killed by a drunk driver. Since Michael presented Maria as his motherless child, Gayle was immediately drawn to her. Here was another child that needed her love and care. She became protective and supportive of Maria.

When Jennifer first appeared in court asking to reinstate her rights, Gayle argued with Jennifer's attorney that she was Maria's mother. Not only did Gayle want to back up Michael and Maria, but the custody fight helped to mask the discomfort and embarrassment Gayle suffered when Michael was again arrested and sentenced for theft and forgery. Gayle gave up her illusions and dreams unwillingly, though Michael had used the alleged trust fund and failed to pay her back.

When Michael and then Maria left Gayle's home, he took not only their belongings, but some of Gayle's as well.

Gayle said her deepest hurt came from the lies Michael told her, but that he also robbed her of money. To this day she lives with the hope that Michael will one day return what is rightfully hers. It is a futile hope.

During her court testimony Gayle said that she truly loved Michael and felt if he had tried they could have worked things out. This told me clearly that she did not yet see Michael as the misogynist that he is. So long as she believed that he would change, he had the ability to manipulate her. She gave him all the power he needed to control the relationship.

And what of Cindy Emery? Luckily for her, she never married Michael, nevertheless, she lived through the same destructive cycles the other women had. During the last days of the relationship and thereafter, she went to counselor after counselor trying to break free of her addiction to Michael. Cindy finally decided the only way she would ever be free of him was to make herself inaccessible. She left her home, her friends, and her family to find peace.

All of us who married or became involved with Michael DeLorenzo lived through disillusionment and pain. Unfortunately, we are not the only women to suffer in this way. There are other Michael DeLorenzos in the world. Some have already preyed on the innocent. Some are poised to attack.

Of course, a child is the most vulnerable and easily wounded of all victims. Despite the utter chaos of her childhood, Maria DeLorenzo has become a beautiful, sensitive young woman. At the age of eighteen, she is working through the difficult memories of her past, is gainfully employed and living independently for the first time.

It is my hope, through the traumatic experiences I have related in this book, to have helped some victims to know that they are not alone and, like the Stellar Star, to warn others of possible danger ahead.

Bibliography

Arcana, Judith. *Every Mother's Son: The Role of Mothers in the Making of Men.* Seattle: Seal Press, 1984.

Chesler, Phyllis. *Mothers on Trial: The Battle for Children and Custody.* Seattle: Seal Press, 1987.

Cowen, Connell, and Kinder, Melvyn. *Smart Women, Foolish Choices: Finding the Right Men and Avoiding the Wrong Ones.* New York: Crown, 1985.

Dowling, Colette. *The Cinderella Complex: Women's Hidden Fear of Independence.* New York: Summit Books, 1981.

Forward, Dr. Susan, and Torres, Joan. *Men Who Hate Women and the Women Who Love Them.* New York: Bantam Books, 1986.

Gordon, Barbara. *I'm Dancing As Fast As I Can.* New York: Harper and Row, 1979.

Halpern, Howard M., Ph.D. *How To Break Your Addiction To A Person.* New York: Bantam Books, 1983.

NiCarthy, Ginny. *Getting Free: A Handbook for Women in Abusive Relationships.* Seattle: Seal Press, 1989.

NiCarthy, Ginny, and Davidson, Sue. *You Can Be Free.* Seattle: Seal Press, 1989.

White, Evelyn C. *Chain, Chain, Change: For Black Women Dealing with Physical and Emotional Abuse.* Seattle: Seal Press, 1985.

Zambrano, Myrna. *Mejor Sola Que Mal Acompanada: For the Latina in an Abusive Relationship/Para la Mujer Golpeada.* Seattle: Seal Press, 1985.